Our Only Hope

K.R. Mele

Copyright © 2019 Rock and Roll Ministries

All rights reserved. No portion of this book may be reproduced, stored in a retrieval system, or transmitted in any form or by any means—electronic, mechanical, photocopy, recording, scanning, or other—except for brief quotations in reviews or articles, without the prior written permission of the author.

Published by Rock and Roll Ministries. Visit www.rocknrollministries.com for more information on bulk discounts and special promotions, or e-mail your questions to krmele@rocknrollministries.com.

Scripture quotations marked NKJV are taken from the New King James Version®. Copyright © 1982 by Thomas Nelson. Used by permission. All rights reserved.

Cover Design: Austin P. Findley
Interior Design: James J. Holden

Subject Headings:

1. Christian life 2. Christianity 3. Bicycle Touring 4. Cycling

ISBN 978-1-7333637-0-9

ISBN 978-1-7333637-1-6 (ebook)

Printed in the United States of America

DEDICATION

Dedicated to the "Mission 66 Team" who responded "yes" to the calling to reach people for Jesus Christ and get our kicks on Route 66.

A special thanks to those who helped along the way...family, friends, pastors, congregations, and the kindness of so many who blessed us as we pedaled from Chicago to Santa Monica. Mostly, thank you to our Lord and Savior, Jesus Christ, who deserves all the glory, honor and praise for what you're about to read.

CONTENTS

	Introduction	7
1.	Feeling Foolish and Weak?	15
2.	Three Years in the Making	23
3.	The Windy City…Here We Go!	33
4.	St. Louis, Missouri	43
5.	Kansas to Oklahoma	63
6.	Texas…Half Way There!	83
7.	New Mexico…Finding Rest	89
8.	Arizona…Almost There!	109
9.	California Here We Come!	121
10.	Conclusion-"You Were On A Mission, Right?"	139

Bible Study For Small Groups

Introduction-2 Chronicles 7:14…"If and Then"	145
Lesson One-If We…*Humble Ourselves*	155
Lesson Two-If We…*Pray*	161
Lesson Three-If We…*Seek His Face*	167
Lesson Four-If We…*Turn From Our Wicked Ways*	173
Lesson Five-Then He Will…*Hear From Heaven*	177
Lesson Six-Then He Will…*Forgive Our Sin*	183
Lesson Seven-Then He Will…*Heal Our Land*	189
About the Author	195

MISSION 66 TEAM

What can I say? When I first shared the vision of Mission 66, I had no idea who would catch the vision and run, or should I say, pedal with it. Some of these people I did not even know.

There are so many things I could say about each member of this team.

Ralph and Sherie, your commitment to this mission was beyond what I ever expected. From buying a camper, to then needing a larger truck to pull the camper, to leaving home for six weeks to taking care of us every single day. Thank you is not enough!

Austin, since you had never been further West than Ohio, this was a big step! Your expertise and catching the whole trip on video and photography was extraordinary. Hopefully it was a life changing experience that provided an opportunity to use your gifts. Your talent is amazing! Use it for His glory.

Zeljko (biker) and Hilda, what can I say? I've never seen a couple nearing eighty years old do what you guys did for a month straight. It's the stuff you read about in the Bible of those that in their old age accomplished much for the Lord. Thanks guys…you inspired us all!

Our Only Hope

Karel, what a blessing it was to meet you and have you with us the first week. In your humbleness and quietness, you spoke volumes. Your servant's heart was such a blessing to have with us...I only wish you could've stayed the entire trip. Thanks, Karel.

Brian (biker) and Melissa, I know this was a stretch for you, Brian, to take this amount of time off from work. But it was great to see Melissa join you on the journey and watch the two of you work together as a team. Thanks for your obedience to follow His calling and stepping out in faith, even when it was hard. And Melissa, thanks for the great food and snacks you provided for the team and being a great support team member.

Bikers...

Dalton, I would have to say I watched you improve physically every single day over the thirty-day ride. Way to go, thanks for taking the challenge and stepping out in faith...and for the good laugh the day you got stuck by yourself out in a downpour!

Joel, by far the strongest one on the team, but also the one with the most flat tires! Thanks for your quiet strength and determination to keep going after each flat tire. As you know, even though they slowed you down, they usually came with a divine appointment right around the corner.

Lloyd, or should I say, *"Crazy Lloyd."* The man who would leave sometimes hours before everyone else to try and get as many miles in as possible and meet people along the way early in the morning. Thanks for your willingness to join the team and share Jesus as you met people in the most unusual places.

Bruce, you were a blessing to have with us the first week of the trip. You were willing to help in whatever way that you could and were determined to do even more miles on your bike than you thought possible. Thanks for your commitment to the team.

Todd, what a blessing to have you join us for the last week of the trip and end it on your birthday. Who would've thought you would do a century plus on your bike on your birthday as you ended with

Introduction

your tires in the Pacific Ocean. Thanks for joining the team and for sharing Jesus with people along the way. Oh, and thanks for providing us with the fuel to keep going as we got our mornings started with the coffee you provided for the team!

Gary, you've been a good friend for many years and it was such a blessing to have you with us for a week. I bet you were wondering what you were getting yourself into those first couple days. You added so much laughter to the trip and it was a blessing to see you take to heart the message we carried and look for ways to share it with others. Thanks for the laughs...thanks for your friendship.

PE News Article

Mission 66 on Route 66
Dan Van Veen

It may be one of the most fascinating and diverse group of cyclists anyone traveling the "Mother Road" of Route 66 could ever hope to encounter — a Canadian evangelist, a 79-year-old Olympic qualifier from the former Yugoslavia, a Ph.D. student from the Congo, some members of the Pentecostal Church of Canada, and a mixture of men and women of various ages from the Family Life church of Penns Valley, Pennsylvania, all led by an AG pastor who once biked across the United States for missions with his longest outdoor training ride only being 26 miles!

However, the *"Mission 66 . . . If My People"* ride from Chicago to Santa Monica, California, taking place Sept. 6 – Oct. 7, isn't about raising funds or to see how fast it can be accomplished. According to K. R. Mele, pastor of Family Life — who learned some valuable lessons on his cross-country bike ride several years ago — this ride is about praying for America and calling people back to God.

"*We chose Route 66 because it was the old road and symbolic of our* desire to see America to return to the old way of thinking — a return to biblical values," Mele says. The Scripture that inspires the ride is 2 Chronicles 7:14, which states: *"If my people, who are called by my name will humble themselves, and pray and seek my face, and turn from their wicked ways, then I will hear from heaven, and will forgive their sin, and heal their land."*

It might be hard to imagine how riding a bicycle could impact lives for Christ, but God has been answering the group's prayers for *"divine encounters"* all along the way.

"We've given out hundreds of Mission 66 tracts and prayed with so many people," Mele says.

Lloyd Vandenberg, a Pentecostal evangelist for the past 32 years from Paris, Ontario, says the ride is a sabbatical for him, but also an opportunity for God to use him in unexpected ways. He says he began talking with a young woman during a stop at a convenience store. She had fallen away from God. *"I asked her if she would like to rededicate her life to the Lord,"* Vandenberg recalls. *"She asked me, 'How do I do that?'"* Shortly after, he led her to the Lord in prayer.

The ride team is currently made up of six riders and a four-person support team who provides food, water, and carries supply for the trip. Most of the riders sleep in a tent or hammock along the way, though if indoor accommodations are offered by a local church, they gladly accept. Austin Findley, is the group's videographer, documenting the journey and posting videos and pictures on the Mission 66 Facebook page.

Mele, who makes daily posts to the Facebook page about their experiences on the ride, shares in those posts about multiple encounters with people who they have been able to present a tract to, pray with, and even lead some in prayer to accept Christ as their Lord and Savior.

But the impact the team is making isn't limited to those calling the central and southwestern portions of the United States home. *"Many people travel this road and stop at all the points of interest,"* Mele explains in one post. *"I was able to meet and give a 'Mission 66' tract to*

Introduction

people from England today . . . and Italy yesterday. What a blessing to meet people from all over the world."

The team varies in size as the ride progresses as not everyone has the time or stamina to ride the full distance. Riding six days a week, the group averages about 88 miles a day, not including Sundays. On Sundays, they don't ride, but instead have ministry engagements at AG churches along the Route 66 path.

One rider that can't help but catch a person's attention — or ear — is Zeljko Pocupec. A 79-year-old who immigrated to Canada from the former Yugoslavia (now Croatia), Pocupec has a heavy and interesting Croatian/Canadian accent. But despite his age and rocking walk, he is a powerful rider. Mele says that Pocupec frequently leads the team in topping hills. But he does have an advantage over all the other riders — his father was an Olympian in 1936 and he himself qualified for the Canadian Olympic Cycling team in his younger years.

For most of the ride, the team has been blessed with good riding weather, although recently the temperatures have started to heat up. But the team is committed to completing the ride and sharing Christ and their mission with those they encounter. It doesn't matter if they meet someone in a store, at a rest stop, or along the roadside, that person is destined to hear about Mission 66, Christ, and offered prayer.

"It's been exciting to see lives changed," Mele says.

Chapter 1
Feeling Foolish and Weak?

The year was 2014, Harold Morgan and I were just completing a missions trip on bike from the pier in Santa Monica, California to the shores of St. Augustine, Florida. We began with our back tire in the Pacific Ocean and thirty-eight days later we were dipping our front tires in the Atlantic. I remember Harold and I looking out at the Atlantic Ocean, kneeling and thanking the Lord, and then simply wondering to ourselves, *"Did that just happen?"*

    The thought swirled around in our minds as we contemplated what just took place and how we seriously could take none of the credit for what unfolded these past 38 days. I mean, my longest ride on a bike had been 26 miles and Harold was 74 years old! We were not likely characters to be doing such a thing. Oh, we may have been *"characters,"* but not ones you would choose to bike from coast to coast. It reminded me of the verse the apostle Paul wrote to those in the Corinthian church:

> *But God has chosen the foolish things of the world to put to shame the wise, and God has chosen the weak things of the world to put to shame the things which are mighty.*
> *-1 Corinthians 1:27*

Our Only Hope

Yep, *"foolish and weak,"* that's us! In the book, *"Don't Quit,"* I write about the many challenges we faced as we embarked on the journey of a lifetime called, *"Coast 2 Coast 4 Jesus."* It was thrilling, it was demanding, it was exciting, it was exhilarating, it was surreal, it was every emotion you can think of wrapped up in one thirty-eight day package. And it was, what I thought, a once in a lifetime opportunity.

That's why when we were nearing the St. Augustine shores and my wife's sister, Robin, who had been following the journey on social media asked, *"When are you going to do this again?",* I couldn't decide to either choke on my water bottle or fall off my bike in laughter. Well, at least inside of me I was laughing. I mean, come on, do this again!? Are you serious? You've got to be crazy, right? All these thoughts came to mind, as my only desire at the moment was to not have to climb on that hard bicycle seat anytime in the near future. To be honest, if this whole thing were just about biking, I wouldn't last very long. That journey, and the one we're about to embark on was always about the *"message"* not the *"miles."* So much more about the *"people,"* not our *"pedals."*

The laughing inside of me at her question made me think of Sarah when she laughed inside when she heard she was going to be pregnant and give birth to a son…at 90! Remember?

> *So Abraham hurried into the tent to Sarah and said, "Quickly, make ready three measures of fine meal; knead it and make cakes." And Abraham ran to the herd, took a tender and good calf, gave it to a young man, and he hastened to prepare it. So he took butter and milk and the calf which he had prepared, and set it before them; and he stood by them under the tree as they ate.*
>
> *Then they said to him, "Where is Sarah your wife?"*
>
> *So he said, "Here, in the tent."*
>
> *And He said, "I will certainly return to you according to the time of life, and behold, Sarah your wife shall have a son."*

Feeling Foolish And Weak

(Sarah was listening in the tent door which was behind him.) Now Abraham and Sarah were old, well advanced in age; and Sarah had passed the age of childbearing. Therefore Sarah laughed within herself, saying, "After I have grown old, shall I have pleasure, my lord being old also?"

And the Lord said to Abraham, "Why did Sarah laugh, saying, 'Shall I surely bear a child, since I am old?' Is anything too hard for the Lord? At the appointed time I will return to you, according to the time of life, and Sarah shall have a son."

But Sarah denied it, saying, "I did not laugh," for she was afraid.

And He said, "No, but you did laugh!" -Genesis 18:6-15

Sarah had to feel both *"foolish and weak."* "Really, at ninety years old I'm going to now have a baby?" Ladies, how would you respond? Yippee!? I mean, just the other day I joked with my wife when I said, *"Wouldn't it be neat if you got pregnant again?"* At fifty-one, she didn't think that would be too *"neat."* I guess men and women see things much differently. But Sarah not only had to carry a baby for nine months, but then she had to give birth...at ninety! Foolish and weak? You better believe it.

The thought of doing another bike trip of serious length was the furthest thing from my mind. Although I did enjoy the bike, the thought of doing something of this distance again – no thank you!

But when I got back home to Centre Hall, Pennsylvania, the Lord began to stir my heart again for another journey. Something that I've learned along the way was that if God places something on your heart to do, you better follow through and do it. If not, later in life you may have many regrets. The key though, is being sure it is the Lord and not just some crazy, hair-brained idea that we come up with on our own. Is it a good idea or a God idea? We must be sure. Questions that I had to answer about another possible mission trip on a bike included:

Our Only Hope

"Why would the Lord want me to do this again? WHY?"

"What would be the reason for this journey?"

"When would this take place?"

"Who would actually join me on the trip?"

The first question that had to be answered was, *"Why?"* It really doesn't matter how crazy or unusual something sounds, the real question becomes, *"Why am I doing it and has the Lord truly called me to do so?"* To be honest, this takes some serious soul searching and time seeking the Lord for direction and wisdom. Again, this had to be more than just a bike ride. Don't get me wrong, I enjoy riding 20, 30 or even 40 miles. But when you get past 50, 70, 90…it's not so enjoyable, especially after day 21 or so. At least not for this guy! Answering this question, *"Why?"* became the very first thing I had to confirm in my heart.

The things we do need to have a deeper purpose than just fulfilling some goal we set only for ourselves.

Jesus lived in a way that was always *"other focused."* If our lives only become about fulfilling our desires and wants, we can quickly become very *"self-focused"* individuals. We will go from one high to another, one adventure to the next and as Solomon puts it, **"chase after the wind"** all our days. The reason for our very existence in life was meant to be greater than this. So *"why"* do we exist?

We were made to glorify God with our lives and then allow Him to use us in whatever way He chooses to reach more people with His love, grace and offer of salvation through His Son, Jesus Christ.

The thing that usually gets in the way of this happening is our self. May we learn to pray like John the Baptist, when he spoke about his relationship to Jesus.

He must increase, but I must decrease. -John 3:30

Or like the Apostle Paul wrote to the Galatians,

Feeling Foolish And Weak

I have been crucified with Christ; it is no longer I who live, but Christ lives in me… -Galatians 2:20

Will those things the Lord asks you to do seem crazy, foolish, outlandish? Will you feel weak at times? Will it seem impossible? Well - if it's from the Lord, most likely, yes! But remember what the Lord reminded Abraham when He asked the question, *"Is anything too hard for the Lord?"*. If you take a glance through the pages of your Bible, you will find people whom the Lord called that felt very inadequate and I'm sure at times extremely foolish. Here are just a few to think about.

- **Noah** *sawing logs and pounding away for 120 years building an ark when it had never before rained.*
- **Sarah** *carrying and delivering a baby at 90…and* **Abraham** *being a father at 100.*
- **Joshua** *walking around the walls of Jericho seven times with men holding trumpets, jars and torches…really?*
- **Ruth** *following Naomi into a foreign land.*
- **Gideon** *having his army dwindle from 32,000 to 300 men and the Lord using them to defeat the Midianites with trumpets, empty pitchers and torches inside. I said "trumpets, empty pitchers and torches…."*
- **David** *with a slingshot and five stones. Yep, a slingshot!*
- **Peter** *stepping out of the boat.*
- **Jesus** *hanging on a cross…*

None of this makes sense, it seems so foolish. Right?

> **But God has chosen the foolish things of the world to put to shame the wise, and God has chosen the weak things of the world to put to shame the things which are mighty. -1 Corinthians 1:27**

Why does God like to work in these ways? He takes ordinary people and uses them in extraordinary ways *so that others will see*

Christ working in them and then He receives the glory for it, not us. Look at the verses that follow these two above.

> ***that no flesh should glory in His presence.***
> ***-1 Corinthians 1:29***

> ***He who glories, let him glory in the Lord.***
> ***-1 Corinthians 1:31***

When we feel the Lord wanting to use us in some way, never forget that even the smallest things can make huge impacts for Christ. You may feel foolish baking your neighbor a pie, shoveling someone's sidewalk, helping someone who is homeless, paying for someone's groceries at the store, or visiting an elderly person at the nursing home. You see, it's not how "*big or small*" something is, but rather the heart motive behind what we do. May we not do things to be seen by men, but rather do what He calls us to do and give Him all the praise for it. I think of the poor widow who gave "*two mites*" and Jesus said she gave much more than those who had given out of their abundance. They both were seen by Jesus and they both gave. But the difference was their heart. It's challenging, but we must always check our hearts to see if they are in the right place in whatever we do. Jesus wants to use us for His glory to see lives reached because as it says in 2 Peter 3:9,

> ***(Jesus is) …not willing that any should perish but that all should come to repentance.***

One key in finding and knowing what the Lord would have us to do begins when we come to grips with how Jesus answered a question posed to Him in Mark 12:28-29.

> ***"Which is the first (greatest) commandment of all?"***

If we can grasp in our hearts the meaning of how Jesus responded to this, it will change how we live and what we do with our days. Jesus answered,

> ***"The first of all the commandments is: Hear, O Israel, the Lord our God, the Lord is one."***

Feeling Foolish And Weak

Most of the time we jump over this part of the verse and right into the *"two greatest commandments"* that Jesus gave. But we can't fulfill these until we respond to what Jesus said first. The phrase Jesus used first challenges me to the core,

> *…the Lord our God, the Lord is one.*

The Lord is One? I have to stop and ask myself the question, *"is there really only One Lord, one God in my life?"* You see, until Christ occupies first place and is the only *"Lord"* in my life, it is impossible for me to fulfill the two greatest commandments Jesus speaks of following this declaration that *"the Lord is one."* Even the Israelites knew this because the very first commandment in Exodus 20:3 states,

> **You shall have no other gods before Me.**

That is a tough question to answer, *"Is the Lord really first in my life, above all else?"* If we truly set apart the Lord Jesus Christ as our One True God, the two greatest commandments that fulfills all the others will begin to capture our hearts and change the way we live. Here is what Jesus said following His statement in the Gospel of Mark,

> *And you shall love the LORD your God with all your heart, with all your soul, with all your mind, and with all your strength.' This is the first commandment. And the second, like it, is this: 'You shall love your neighbor as yourself.' There is no other commandment greater than these."*
> *-Mark 12:30, 31*

Hmm…riding across Route 66 on another mission trip? Sounds a little bit crazy. With a team this time? Lord, you have to be in the midst of this. You have to be the One directing this. Like Moses said to the Lord in Exodus 33:15,

> *If Your Presence does not go with us, do not bring us up from here.*

Oh, Lord, if Your Presence does not go with us, I really don't want any part of this.

CHAPTER 2
THREE YEARS IN THE MAKING

In September 2014, about three months following the "*Coast 2 Coast 4 Jesus*" trip, the Lord began to birth another vision in my heart to take a team of bikers with me on Route 66 and call it "*Mission 66...If My People.*" In seeing the desperate need in our country, I began to pray, journal and seek the Lord for His wisdom and a team of people to catch this vision for revival in our country and in our churches.

The vision was simple, we would take the message from 2 Chronicles 7:14 on a mission along Route 66, typically referred to as the "*Main Street of America*." This message would not only be for our country, but especially for those who call themselves Christian. I truly believe that the reason America has spiraled downward over the past several decades is because we have abandoned Christ and the Word of God. Not only our country, but many who refer to themselves as Christian.

> *If My people who are called by My name will humble themselves, and pray and seek My face, and turn from their wicked ways, then I will hear from heaven, and will forgive their sin and heal their land.* -2 Chronicles 7:14

This verse is clearly directed towards God's people. I will direct my attention to the background of this verse in the second half of book. But first, we must recognize that *"if My people"* refers to God's people. We are the ones that must humble ourselves, pray, seek His face and turn from our wicked ways. If we do, then and only then will God hear from heaven, forgive our sin and heal our land. Revival begins when God's people begin to seek Him, not when the world or our government gets it right first.

To help explain what I'm saying, let's take a look at the third commandment found in Exodus 20:7.

> ***You shall not take the name of the LORD your God in vain, for the LORD will not hold him guiltless who takes His name in vain.***

Most often we immediately think of someone swearing or using the name of the Lord in an inappropriate way when we say to *"not use the name of the Lord God in vain."* Now - we all know that it's wrong to use God's name in a vulgar manner. But let's also look at the context of this verse from Exodus in this way.

When we become a follower of Jesus Christ, we *"take on His Name."* We begin to call ourselves a Christian, something we didn't do prior to this moment. When we call ourselves by His Name, but then live in ways that misrepresent Christ, are we not *"taking His name in vain?"* I don't know about you, but when I talk with people who *"don't go to church"*, there are two reasons I find most stay home and far away from that building we call *"church."*

One is they say, *"they just want my money."* The second, *"they're just a bunch of hypocrites."* Some people respond to that second statement with, *"Oh, well come on along then - what's one more?"* No, we are not to live like hypocrites because Jesus was very hard on the *"religious"* of his day who said one thing and lived a completely other way. He even called them by what they actually were - hypocrites!

> ***But woe to you, scribes and Pharisees, hypocrites! For you shut up the kingdom of heaven against men; for you***

> *neither go in yourselves, nor do you allow those who are entering to go in. -Matthew 23:13*

Even John wrote about this in one of his small books.

> *Now by this we know that we know Him, if we keep His commandments. He who says, "I know Him," and does not keep His commandments, is a liar, and the truth is not in him. -1 John 2:3, 4*

Now think about what Jesus said were the two greatest commandments: To love the Lord your God with all your heart, soul, mind and strength and to love your neighbor as yourself. When we do these two things, we are no longer living hypocritically, but rather like Christ.

So the message we took with us was *"Mission 66...If My People,"* was a message to call God's people (Christ's Followers) back to Biblical living. To live according to God's Word.

Here is a peek into some of my journal entries I recorded as the Lord continued to confirm this vision in my heart.

September 13th, 2014

The last couple days I've been thinking and now praying about a mission team that would join me on a bike trek from Chicago to Santa Monica on Old Route 66. Just like Route 66 has been around a long time and would carry people from one place to another, so is the plan of salvation through His Son, Jesus Christ, that will carry us someday from this earth to heaven.

This mission trip would remind people to return to God's ways before it's too late. There will be an end in sight on this bike trip, the pier in Santa Monica. But unless America returns to the Lord and Biblical values, the discipline and downfall of our nation will be in our future.

My desire for this journey is to call people back to the Bible and the Godly principles found in the Scriptures. It is our only hope as a nation and individually as His people. Please show me Lord if this is to be Your will once again. Thank you for your Holy Spirit that will guide me in the days that follow.

October, 2014

Dr. George Wood, in his "Called to Serve" article to Assembly of God pastors, states, "If there ever was a time we need to take seriously the challenge of 2 Chronicles 7:14, it is now!"[1]

January 22, 2015

The more I think and pray about this mission, the more I feel His Spirit continuing to move me forward.

April 11, 2015

The desire to assemble a team to go on "Mission 66" continues to increase. I read this morning from 2 Chronicles 34 and it reminded me of how America has also forgotten what the Book says and how we must find it again if we want our country to be saved from destruction.

April 22, 2015

As I sit here in Los Angeles, one year following our first bike trip, reminiscing is easy to do. Would I do it again? Absolutely! I'm looking forward to pursuing "Mission 66" with a team of people to spread the message that our country desperately needs to hear - Repentance that Leads to Revival.

July 22, 2015

Mission 66 becomes more of a reality as I pray about it. Even now Lord, bring a team together for this purpose.

It's been about a year since my initial journal entry when I shared this vision with my wife. I've learned over time to really spend time in prayer before just blurting out that you're going to do something. Too many times I've opened my mouth before thinking. Maybe you can relate to this as well. May I encourage you that when you sense the Lord wanting you to do something, just begin to pray, seek the

Lord, journal and repeat this day after day. If that burden continues to grow and doesn't leave your heart, you'll know it's Him and not just something you ate the night before.

December 31, 2015

The more I see the moral decay of our country, the more my heart becomes sad and the reason I feel we must go proclaim this truth, "If My People…" Oh, Lord, continue to show me and confirm in my heart if this ride in 2017 would be Your will. For tomorrow (1.1.16), I would be saying, "that's next year."

January 27, 2016

After speaking in chapel at the University of Valley Forge, Dr. Meyer shared a thought that should have been so obvious to me, but wasn't. But, oh, how it fits with "Mission 66…If My People." He said, "The Bible has 66 books in it!" Wow…so simple, yet so profound.

Later that year, I would share this vision with our congregation. I felt that if I took the first step of faith, that the Lord would *"fill in the blanks"* along the way. So, in faith, I set a date for our first meeting. I had to simply trust that He would bring the right group of people together to become a part of the Mission 66 team.

Fast forward to 2017 as we rapidly move closer to our starting point in Chicago, Illinois…Grant Park by the waters of Lake Michigan.

May 12, 2017

Only 114 days until we take the message, "If My People…" with us onto the "Main Street of America." I glanced back in my journal to see what I was doing three years ago today on the first trip, "Coast 2 Coast 4 Jesus."

It just so happens that exactly three years ago I was completing my first 100 mile day! Could it really be three years ago that took place? 114 days will be here before I know it.

I remember while on that bike trip, someone asked me, "When are you going to do this again?" And I thought, "Are you crazy?" Well, turns out maybe I'm the one that's crazy. But that won't be the first time because my wife has referred to me in that way many times over the past twenty nine years of marriage.

I really never thought I would've done this again, but when the Lord keeps stirring your heart, it's either obey or live wondering what would've happened if you had done so. Jeremiah 29:11 reminds us that He knows our plans. We must listen to His voice and obey His Word to find His will. Proverbs 16:9 says that **"A man's heart plans his way, but the Lord directs his steps."**

So, this vision, "Mission 66" has been a plan in my heart for some time now, and I'm asking You Lord to direct our steps as we prepare for this journey ahead. The team is about set. This will be much different from our last journey. Then we had two bikers and two on the support team with a van. We stayed in either motels, hotels, churches or with friends.

This trip looks like there will be 4 or 5 bikers riding all 2,499 miles from Chicago to Santa Monica with a few other riders possibly joining us for a week or so of the trip. An RV will be our housing with a husband/wife team setting up each night for accommodations and also hopefully a support vehicle near us as we bike. This trip has many more details to work out, but I'm very thankful for the unique team that the Lord is bringing together to accomplish His will on "Mission 66."

May 13, 2017

My mind keeps drifting toward the need we have for a support vehicle team. My heart keeps leaning toward an older couple, husband/wife, that would be able to join us. Lord, you know the perfect team that is to form together. Like everything else, I give this need to You and ask that You confirm in my heart who is supposed to join us in this vital role for the Mission 66 journey.

May 15, 2017

Please open up the right doors for churches to stay with and share the message, "Our Only Hope."

May 17, 2017

Found some great airline tickets out of State College for the team. We'll find out today who is really on board with this trip.

May 18, 2017

What a deal! I ordered tickets to fly from State College to Chicago for some of the team, but did something I had never done before to save time and money. A flight from State College to Chicago would've had a layover in Detroit and cost over $200. So I put in a flight from State College to Detroit, and wouldn't you know that they had a layover in Chicago? The cost was $142 and we just won't take the second leg of the flight and hop off in Chicago. I thank the Lord for His provision. (Currently some airlines have issue with this – but then – no problem!)

May 22, 2017

I continue to stand amazed as I watch the Lord bring together the perfect team for such a time as this. Lloyd Vandenberg called yesterday to say he is in for the entire trip. Todd Pugh also messaged to say he is 95% in for one of the segments and Ryan Grabill is going to ride with us from St. Louis to Springfield (this would change later due to Ryan, who serves with Convoy of Hope, needing to respond to disaster relief from hurricane Harvey that hit Houston).

We still need a support vehicle team, but I know You are also going to provide the perfect ones for this need as well. Thank you, Jesus, for always hearing, knowing and taking our needs before our Heavenly Father. For your Word says that you live and intercede for us everyday (Hebrews 7:25).

May 25, 2017

We've connected with three congregations along the trip and it looks like two of them will have me share the message, "Our Only Hope." Thank you, Lord, that You are the One leading and guiding this team. May we be still and quiet enough to hear Your voice (Psalm 46:10).

May 30, 2017

100 day countdown begins today! As I sit here this morning, I'm reminded of the message from 2 Chronicles, "If My People" that we will be carrying with us on this journey. I believe it is a message that can turn our country back to the Lord. A message of repentance, renewal and revival.

Lord, be stirring the hearts of the team members to boldly proclaim this message as we prepare and in just 100 days begin pedaling our way from Chicago to Santa Monica. Even now Lord Jesus, prepare the people we're to meet, the congregations we're to speak to and the opportunities You'll give us to be used as Your mouthpiece.

Oh Lord, stir our hearts, prepare our lives for this journey…and may You receive all the glory, honor and praise!

Random Journal Entries leading up to September 6th

-May Your Holy Spirit begin and continue to stir the waters so that America turns their hearts back to You…Oh Lord, send revival!

-I know You are working in ways I do not know or cannot see for a support team to begin the trip.

-Less than 70 days until we leave with the message "If My People" on our bikes.

Under 50 days…hard to believe! The team has grown and shrunk as well. Bruce, and also Lloyd's friends Zjelko and Hilda will be joining us, but it looks as though Earl's family won't be able to make the journey.

-Zjelko and Hilda are another answer to prayer. We needed a support vehicle driver and the Lord provided. Zjelko is 78, will turn 79 in October, and has a passion to bike the entire trip….as he says, "God willing." He reminds me of Caleb, who at 85 said, "Give me this mountain" (Joshua 14:6-12). I've only spoken to this couple by phone, but I look forward to meeting them in Chicago in 26 days.

-Exactly three weeks and we'll be in Grant Park at the Buckingham Fountain in Chicago! Just seems like yesterday it was 3 months to go and also 3 years ago since completing "Coast 2 Coast 4 Jesus." Reminds me of what James compares life to when he asks the question, "What is your life?" He goes on to tells us, ***"It is even a vapor that appears for a little time and then vanishes away." James 4:14***

-The last two days have been amazing to watch You open doors for places to stay, churches to connect with and even receive supplemental vitamins from a company for the entire team. I love walking this out because it really causes me to trust You with details that still need to be secured. Two weeks from today we will pedal away from Grant Park in Chicago. Lord, continue to prepare the way and especially the people's hearts we're about to meet.

September 5, 2017

Well…it's real! Do you ever plan for something that seems so far away, and then, "bam," it's here? It's been about a year since we started praying, planning and preparing for this trip. Ralph, Sherie, Austin, Dalton and Bruce began the trek towards Chicago yesterday. Zeljko, Hilda, Lloyd, Karel, Brian, Joel and I will head to Chicago today. Lord, safety for all and divine appointments along the way. As it says in Proverbs 16:9, "direct our steps." I truly ask that You and You alone receive all glory, honor and praise. Here we go…go with us, Lord Jesus. For if you don't go before us, we might as well not go at all.

Our Only Hope

Lord, You know every person were about to meet. Prepare us, prepare them...have Your way.

Wow, I just gave a letter to Brian that his wife wanted me to give to him on the plane. He handed it to me to read after he did, what a letter! The one thing I remember her saying was "how she has never been more proud of him." What words to hear from your wife.

Gina had prayed this morning a verse that I read this morning from Proverbs 16:9... "Lord, direct their steps." Oh, Lord do so...lead us every step of this journey...all for Your glory. Boy, I miss her already. It will be a very long thirty-two days without the one I love.

Thank you for the privilege to do what were about to do.

Let's enjoy the journey!

CHAPTER 3
THE WINDY CITY...HERE WE GO!

Boom! Divine Appointment #1

Having arrived in Chicago, Joel, Brian and I made it to Belmont Assembly of God, where we would spend our first night. The rest of the team was still on their way and some even enjoyed *"Deep Dish Chicago Style Pizza."* Even the sound of that right now makes my mouth water. I love to find small pizza joints in towns and grab a couple slices and a Coke. Having never been to Chicago, deep dish pizza sounded perfect for dinner. Unfortunately, there were no pizza joints to be found near the church! So, we settled for one of my other favorite foods, Mexican.

We weren't too sure about this place, but it was fantastic, and it's exactly where the Lord wanted us to be. We asked our server, Domingo, if there was anything we could pray for before we enjoyed our meal. He mentioned how he lives here while his wife and three children reside in Mexico. They've been apart for the past eight years.

As I went to pay our bill, I asked if I could pray for him and his family, which he gladly agreed to and was thankful to receive. Domingo is one I will remember to pray for as we pedal away from the Windy City tomorrow. Let's just hope and pray that the wind is behind our backs, unlike that second day in CA on our Coast 2 Coast 4 Jesus trip…

I believe the Lord has divine appointments awaiting us every day we leave our front door. Maybe it's a co-worker, someone who serves us a meal, the bank teller or a host of other people that the Lord puts in our path during the course of any given day. We would find that to be the case the very next morning…and the next thirty-two days ahead as well.

Day 1 – September 6th

September 6th, could it really be? We've anticipated this day for quite some time now. With so much on my mind as we begin this journey in the morning, sleep would be very scarce tonight. We crashed in a big open fellowship hall. Some slept on air mattresses, some on the floor, some on several chairs that they slid together. And then there was one from our team who found a nice cozy couch in one of the pastors' offices…. Needless to say, we were thankful for a roof over our heads, and a place to lie down.

But sleep would not come easy tonight as my eyes only remained closed from about 11:00 PM-2:00 AM. I tried to catch a few more ZZZs, but I finally gave up the fight around 4:00 AM and rolled out

The Windy City...Here We Go!

of my sleeping bag to begin Day #1. Catching just a few hours of sleep was not the best way to begin the journey.

We left the church around 6:30am and arrived in Grant Park by 7:15am. What a place to begin as we dipped our back tires in Lake Michigan! But our beginning had an interesting twist. You could call it **"Divine appointment #2."**

One of our team members, Lloyd, discovered he had a small leak in his tire right before we were going to begin this 32 day journey. It was frustrating for him to have to change a tube even before the first rotation of his tire. But what I'm about to share reminds me of the verse found in **Isaiah 55:8** that says,

"For my thoughts are not your thoughts, nor are your ways My ways," says the Lord.

Lloyd told us to get started and that he would find the support vehicle, change his flat and catch up with us later. As he repaired his tire and was ready to head towards the team, he was delayed again. Lloyd shared with us how a man simply walked up to him and said, *"I need to get my life straight."*

Lloyd began to talk to this man about the Lord and explain to him about salvation. He offered to pray with him to know Christ in his life and the man agreed to do so. What a way to start our trip... a flat tire that led to a saved life! To think that if Lloyd would not have had that flat, he would've missed this divine appointment from the Lord.

Isn't that how life goes sometimes? A disappointment comes our way at a very inconvenient time, like a flat tire. But if we trust the Lord through those disappointments, He will work **"all things together for good"** *(Romans 8:28)*. When the Lord says, *"all things,"* He means, well, *"all things."* Is it easy to trust Him during these times of disappointment? Not always, especially when it takes much longer than it takes to change a flat tire. But let's look at this verse in its entirety to completely understand what Paul writes here in Romans.

> *And we know that all things work together for good to those who love God, to those who are called according to His purpose.*

We see in this verse that *"all things work together for good"* for who? For those who *"love God."* And also *"to those who are called according to His purpose."*

If you are one who loves God and are walking according to His purpose for your life, you can trust Christ and know that He will *"work together for good"* whatever you may be going through in your life right now. It may not be a quick fix and it may take some time, but here are some verses that Paul wrote to encourage you while you wait for God's perfect timing.

> *Therefore, having been justified by faith, we have peace with God through our Lord Jesus Christ,*
>
> *through whom also we have access by faith into this grace in which we stand, and rejoice in hope of the glory of God.*
>
> *And not only that, but we also glory in tribulations, knowing that tribulation produces perseverance;*
>
> *and perseverance, character; and character, hope.*
>
> *Now hope does not disappoint, because the love of God has been poured out in our hearts by the Holy Spirit who was given to us. -Romans 5:1-5*

We can be confident in knowing that whatever we are walking through, the Lord is developing our character and hope because His love has been poured into our hearts by the Holy Spirit. As a friend of mine said one time, "*We aren't fighting for victory, we're fighting from victory.*" The cross and the resurrection give us everything we need to overcome. It's never easy to *"glory in tribulations."* If it were easy, we would not need Christ, right? Remember what Paul wrote to young Timothy?

The Windy City...Here We Go!

> *You therefore must endure hardship as a good soldier of Jesus Christ. -2 Timothy 2:3*

Let's keep fighting, keep our eyes fixed on Jesus and remember that a good soldier never quits, he fights until the very end. Let's join Paul in saying one day,

> *I have fought the good fight, I have finished the race, I have kept the faith. -2 Timothy 4:7*

This first day of biking out of the Windy City went very well. Everyone completed the 83 miles that we set out to do. One of the highlights for me on the bikes was watching the Lord give strength to our oldest team member, Zjelko, who was just short of turning 79 years old. Many times he was in front blazing the trail for us.

Zjelko is originally from Croatia and he and his wife, Hilda, now reside in Canada. He has been involved in biking over the years for what he says was a *"corruptible crown."* Zjelko gives all the glory to the Lord and now says he is racing for what the Apostle Paul calls an *"incorruptible crown."*

Our support team, Karel and Hilda, were amazing and provided a great lunch and *"mom and dad"* (Ralph & Sherie), had *"ham & beans, potatoes, corn and pasta salad"* waiting for us when we arrived at our temporary-home-for-32-days in Braidwood, Illinois. Our videographer, Austin, ended the day producing an amazing first-day video of the trip, one of many that he would produce over the next month.

Now this seems very real! One down, thirty-one to go.

Day 2 – September 7th

Our second day in Illinois saw us get on the road by around 8:30am, later than we wanted to be. I realize from my last trip across country that it will take several days to get into a groove and feel like we know what we're doing. The winds today were pretty hard against us as we pounded out another 81 miles. There weren't many hills today, just a gradual increase over most of the ride. But more than anything, my heart was full of thanks as I rode on the bike and began to see how the Lord has provided for this trip to happen. Thankful for my family, my congregation back home, and congregations and people that would bless and help us along the way. We even had friends of friends that would connect us with people that we didn't even know that were more than willing to give us a hand.

Friends, from old to new ones, we were very blessed and grateful. A grateful heart is key to being spiritually healthy. The Bible speaks so much about being thankful. Being grateful is a big part of discovering God's will for our lives. Here's how Paul described it to the church in Thessalonica.

> ***Rejoice always, pray without ceasing, in everything give thanks; for this is the will of God in Christ Jesus for you. -1 Thessalonians 5:16-18***

I'm sure that many of you have asked yourself the question, or have had someone ask you the following:

"How do I know God's will for my life?"

Great question, right? But rather than look at *"His will"* as something you have to find, view it as something that will unfold as you're obedient to His Word. The key to finding God's will is to spend time regularly in His Word and allow it to direct your steps. Here are some things the Psalmist reminds us of in Psalm 119.

> *Direct my steps by Your word. -Psalm 119:133(a)*

> *Your word is a lamp to my feet and a light to my path. -Psalm 119:105*

> *I rejoice at Your word as one who finds great treasure. -Psalm 119:162*

> *Your word have I hidden in my heart, that I might not sin against You. -Psalm 119:11*

As we spend time in God's Word, the Holy Spirit will begin to shine His light on our path and make us walk in His ways. His will is not some magical formula or mystery to somehow figure out. His will is found in obedience to His Word. The verse above from 1 Thessalonians 5 told us that there are three things we should be doing that is God's will for our lives. They are:

1) Rejoice always

2) Pray without ceasing

3) In everything give thanks

And then it says....

... for this is the will of God in Christ Jesus for you.

Yes, His will may include who you're to marry, where to attend college, what career path to choose, what city or country to live in, etc. But according to this verse, His will can be discovered as we do these three things: Rejoice, Pray and Give Thanks.

To *"**rejoice always**"* is not easy. But it's in those hard things we go through that we have to remember to rejoice the most. It's easy to rejoice when things are fine. But it's during difficult seasons of life that the enemy wants to bring us down and cause us to stop rejoicing.

Now I'm not saying that we have to go around dancing and singing when we're hurting and going through trials. But deep down inside, we must learn to rejoice, knowing that the Lord is walking with us no matter what we are experiencing at the time. You are never alone when you know Jesus as your Savior and Lord.

"*Praying without ceasing*" is the next part of His will for our lives. If it's not already, begin to make prayer a part of your day, not only when you eat a meal or go to bed. Yes, those times are important. But we must begin to pray about, well, everything.

Does God care about everything going on in our lives? Absolutely! So why not invite Him into every area of our lives, seek Him first and ask for wisdom to make good choices and right decisions?

Our Only Hope

This third part of this verse says, "*in everything give thanks.*" Everything? That's what it says! Notice it doesn't say, "*for everything*," but rather "*in everything give thanks.*" There is a difference. Say your life is experiencing significant pain and suffering due to some things that have happened recently. There is a difference in thanking God *"for"* those things and thanking Him *"in"* those things.

If the enemy tried to bring those things into your life to destroy you, you don't want to be thankful *"for"* them; but rather you want to thank God *"in"* them because once again, He is walking with you through them. He never leaves you alone. Look what Isaiah writes.

> ***When you pass through the waters, I will be with you; And through the rivers, they shall not overflow you. When you walk through the fire, you shall not be burned.***
> ***-Isaiah 43:2***

Notice that He will take you through these things, not leave you stranded in the middle of them. Let's begin to thank Him in the midst of our trials, knowing that He will take us through them to the other side.

I think of how Job didn't thank God that his family was killed and basically lost all that he had. He didn't thank God *"for"* those things that happened, but he continued to hold onto the Lord while *"in"* the things that wanted to destroy him. Don't ever let go of the Lord, don't give up, as I wrote in a previous book, "*don't quit!*" He will sustain you and make sure you make it to the other side.

As we ended the day biking, I reflected on how well the team worked together today. From drafting, to helping one another as we pedaled shoulder to shoulder up a hill. One moment that I'll never forget happened when I came across three workers along the side of the road. Two were in a ditch working and one guy was standing by his truck. I was by myself at the time and decided to stop and talk with this one man.

After some brief introductions, I began to briefly share my testimony with Chad. I mentioned how at the age of 21 I gave my life to Christ, almost 30 years ago. He seemed very interested in what

I was saying and I felt the Lord nudge me to ask him if he would like to know Christ and His forgiveness in his life. He looked at me and said, *"yes."* I had the great privilege to shake his hand and lead him in a prayer of salvation. Praise the Lord; this is why we're here, to spread the Good News of Jesus Christ!

> ***For the Son of Man has come to save that which was lost.***
> ***-Matthew 18:11***

Today, I thank the Lord that Chad was once lost, but has now been found.

Day 3 – September 8th

Today, the team was ready to go and out the door by 8am, which was quite the feat for so many people getting ready at the same time. Most of us slept in the camper, but Bruce made his bed on a cot outside, Brian was in a tent and Dalton would spend the first of many nights sunk into his hammock. One of the highlights for me today had to do with two guys I met along the way.

The first was Joe in Lincoln, Illinois. He was sitting just outside the theatre where he works. As we talked, he began to share with me how his twin brother had died in 2003, then opened up with me about another rough stretch of his life that he had to walk through. During that season though, he came to know the Lord. I've found that to be so true, that when someone has exhausted all other means and have nowhere else to turn, they turn to the Lord. The great news is, He is always there waiting for us!

As Joe shared with me more about his life, I simply reminded him of the importance of being in God's Word consistently. He looked at me, somewhat in amazement, and I wondered if I had somehow offended him. But then he shared with me that just yesterday, his mother-in-law had told him that she wanted to buy him a new Bible.

We were both quite amazed as to how the Lord directed our paths to meet at that very spot on this day. Another divine appointment. And to think if we didn't stop to change another flat tire, we may have never met one another. My conversation with Joe reminded me of the power of God's Word to transform our lives.

> ***All Scripture is given by inspiration of God, and is profitable for doctrine, for reproof, for correction, for instruction in righteousness, that the man of God may be complete, thoroughly equipped for every good work.***
> ***-2 Timothy 3:16, 17***

Elijah would be the next man we met. As Lloyd, Joel and I were on the corner of a street trying to figure out our maps, he went walking by us. As he passed by, the Lord nudged me to go talk with him. So I pedaled down to where he was by now and introduced myself to him.

I began to talk with him about what we were doing and then about what Christ has done for each of us. As we spoke, he began to share with me how his brother had died and how his brother's faith in Christ was very important to him. This was the second man that I met within a couple hours who each had a brother die. I asked Elijah if he had ever believed in Christ himself. I explained to him that if we ask Christ into our lives and believe that He died for our sins, that we can be forgiven and live with Him in Heaven someday. Then I asked him the question...

"Would you like to do so today?"

He said, "*Yes.*"

We extended our hands and joined them together in prayer. He said to me, *"I don't know how to pray, I never have before."* So I had the wonderful privilege to pray with Elijah to ask Christ to forgive him and come into his life and be his Lord and Savior. What a moment! Elijah made my day, when he looked at me after we prayed, and said, *"Thanks, I really needed that."* It was a moment I'll never forget.

CHAPTER 4
ST. LOUIS, MISSOURI

An eighty-five mile day would land us in St. Louis for the night. It would also afford us the privilege of crossing the first state off our list! One down, seven to go…

We would travel over the Mississippi River by way of the "*Chain of Rocks Bridge.*" Today's ride found us on a bike path for almost half of our miles. Bike paths are nice, although you usually don't get to talk with as many people because the ones you do encounter are either running, walking or riding.

Our Only Hope

Lloyd did have an opportunity to pray with one lady for healing and encouraged her to get back to worshipping the Lord in her life.

There was another guy that I had the chance to speak with on the path who shared with me about how at one point in his life he was homeless for 56 days and sat outside a church and read the Bible from cover to cover. One of the great things about a trip of this nature is that it allows you to slow down and just listen to people's stories.

We found an IGA Supermarket for lunch and sat under a tree just beside their parking lot. One of the ladies that worked at the store came out and gave us twenty dollars while we were eating just to help us with our expenses. She was excited for what we were doing. The team continued to experience how the Lord was taking care of all our needs along the way.

As the day came to a close, we arrived at New Hope Fellowship, where Pastor Dan Ross and his congregation welcomed us into their beautiful facility. Since it was Saturday, we would settle in for two nights before heading out Monday morning. Upon our arrival, they had burgers and fries ready for us to eat…what a blessing! We'll get some much needed rest here, worship in the morning, and then pedal away from where we ended Saturday night, at the St. Louis Arch, Monday morning.

Day 5 – September 10th

To fully appreciate what I'm about to say, I must go back to Chicago (and even before) to tell you how meaningful this morning's worship service meant to me. When I go on any type of trip, I like to pick a certain portion of the Bible to read while I'm away. During my days at home, I typically read from Genesis to Revelation. Sometimes when I go away, I like to get out of my normal routine and focus on certain portions of Scripture. There have been times I've picked a few of Paul's letters to read, the book of Romans, or maybe the *"Psalms of*

Ascent" or Proverbs. But as I prayed before leaving on this trip, the Lord impressed on my heart, *"Read the Minor Prophets of the Old Testament."* I asked myself, *"Really, why?"*

So as we boarded the plane in State College to leave for Chicago, I pulled out my Bible and opened to the book of Hosea and began reading Chapter 1. Why in the world would the Lord have me start here? I would soon discover the answer to that question this morning.

As we entered worship this morning, Pastor Dan began his message, *"Unfaithfulness in the Family of God,"* by asking everyone to turn to Hosea, the first minor prophet writing in the Old Testament!

It was exactly where I began my reading for this trip. I can't even remember the last time I heard a preacher preach on this chapter, but it was a confirmation in my heart that we were exactly where the Lord wanted us to be on this trip. His message lined up perfectly with the one we were carrying with us on our bikes.

Pastor Dan gave me a few minutes to share in both services about *"Mission 66"* and a man following the first service came up and gave me a *"Pentecostal handshake."* He simply shook my hand and as he let go, what remained was a hundred dollar bill! He just wanted to help our team with some expenses along the way.

As we closed another day, my mind kept going back to what Zjelko would remind us of everyday on this trip. *"God is good…all the time…and all the time…God is good."*

Day 6 – September 11th

This morning began early as we had to get back to where we ended on Saturday, the Arch in St. Louis. We were about 45 minutes away, so we woke early, enjoyed a good breakfast that Pastor Dan had ready, and then our support van along with a wonderful lady from the church, Mary, helped shuttle us to the Arch in downtown St. Louis.

Driving into a major city on an early Monday morning added some stress to the start of our second week. I found myself having to constantly remind myself of our vision and purpose so that I would not become distracted so easily. Mary would help with this as she prayed for our team before we set off on our bikes. Thank you, Mary!

Isn't this true in life no matter what we are doing? You may be doing something you know the Lord has called you to do, but the enemy keeps trying to distract you with lies, discouragement, and downright deception. We must not allow the enemy to steal our dreams that the Lord has placed in our hearts. He will surely try, but we must constantly remind ourselves that our God is greater!

When we are in the midst of our days, fulfilling God's calling in our lives, there will come opposition. The enemy would be thrilled if we just laid down and quit. But we need to remember the verse that John wrote in one of his small letters.

> ***You are of God, little children, and have overcome them, because He who is in you is greater than he who is in the world. -1 John 4:4***

Maybe you had a dream or vision from God at one point in your life. Maybe the Lord is reminding you of it right now. I encourage you to resurrect that dream that has been dormant for quite some time now. God wants to do a new thing in your life!

> ***I will do a new thing. -Isaiah 43:19***

Shortly after pedaling away from the Arch in St. Louis, the first young man I met was a student at the University of St. Louis. He was walking along the bike path in the opposite direction that I was biking.

As I passed by him, I remember looking at him and our eyes connected. I rode a little further and the Lord spoke to my heart and said, "*Turn around and connect with him.*" As I turned back and found him, I introduced myself to him and discovered he was from China.

I shared the reason for our journey and what we were doing. I began to explain to him not only what we were doing, but more importantly what Christ has done for us. He then explained to me that his sister lives in Hong Kong, goes to church and believes in Jesus. I asked if he had ever trusted in Christ and believed in Him and he said that he never did. I invited him to do so as we talked on that bike path, and as we shook hands, he agreed in prayer with me to ask Christ into his life and begin that journey with Him. What a moment!

I mentioned to him about calling his sister to tell her what happened this morning. It's so important to begin sharing Christ with others as soon as we come to know Him because it confirms in our hearts what just took place and begins to strengthen our faith.

> *...that if you confess with your mouth the Lord Jesus and believe in your heart that God has raised Him from the dead, you will be saved. For with the heart one believes unto righteousness, and with the mouth confession is made unto salvation.* -Romans 10:9, 10

Believing and confessing is the beginning of our relationship with Christ. After believing, the confessing with our mouths means more than just that initial prayer, but rather it means to testify and tell others with your mouth what Christ has done for you and that He is now your Lord and Savior. The more we testify with our mouths, the stronger our faith and walk will become as we testify of what He has done in our lives through His forgiveness and grace.

One thing I found interesting was something this young man said to me. He said that a reason he agreed to pray with me was because "*when I spoke it was slow and he could understand what I was saying.*"

Our Only Hope

This really got me thinking since no one had ever said that to me before. Even though he was specifically referring to the language barrier, how often have we overcomplicated the message of salvation or spoken too quickly for someone to understand the message? It was a good reminder for me to slow down, speak clearly, and not complicate the greatest message ever.

As we said our goodbyes, he said to me with a big grin on his face, *"What a lucky man I was today."* I really knew what he meant, because I felt the same way about meeting him. But luck really had nothing to do with it, only the hand of God. A popular saying we hear these days when someone is going somewhere or is about to face a big task ahead is, *"good luck."* But really, who needs luck when you have the Lord? And to think, I could've missed it all if I had not turned back on my bike, or if we had never left Pennsylvania.

One other conversation that I had today was with a man from Kuwait who spoke very little English. To be honest, I don't know how much he understood of what I was saying, but as I prayed for him, he did say the name "Jesus" with me. I do know this, there is power in the Name of Jesus.

> ***Therefore God also has highly exalted Him and given Him the name which is above every name, that at the name of Jesus every knee should bow, of those in heaven, and of those on earth, and of those under the earth, and that every tongue should confess that Jesus Christ is Lord, to the glory of God the Father. -Philippians 2:9-11***

After I gave him one of the *"Mission 66"* tracts, he went to sit by a young lady who was also from Kuwait. I learned that she was attending a University nearby for her PHD. I invited Joel over to meet and talk with her since Joel is also studying for his PHD at Penn State University. I took a step back and watched and listened as Joel and this lady spoke about their educational experiences.

As I rejoined the conversation, we began to share with her all that Jesus has done for us. It was very interesting that, even though she was not ready to receive Christ into her life, she said, *"I would like to learn more."* Well, we had more! We handed her a Gospel of John and our prayer is that she reads, learns more and comes to place her faith in Christ.

As we got back on our bikes, Lloyd and I came across a man who was in his vehicle on the side of the road. He was waiting for a friend. As we stopped to talk with him, it was such a blessing to encourage him to know the Lord as he prayed to receive Christ into his life.

After praying, he said to us, *"I never prayed anything like that before."* I'm so grateful for all the people the Lord is bringing our way. All have unique stories and situations they find themselves in. But the one thing we all have in common is our need for a Savior.

Our final opportunity for the day came as Lloyd and I rode by a lady who was dragging a huge chair out to the roadside to be thrown away. The chair probably weighed as much as her. I looked back as Lloyd had stopped to help and I wheeled around to give him a hand.

As we began to talk with her, we came to find out that she was divorced and also currently separated from a guy because of an abusive relationship. We talked to her about the hope, love and forgiveness that she can find in Christ. She spoke of how at one time she had given her life to Christ, but then asked a very important question when she said, *"But how do I re-dedicate my life to Him again?"*

Lloyd and I spoke to her about the prodigal son in the Bible who came back home. We shared with her how the Lord is waiting, watching for her to come back home, into His arms. And as she began to pray with us, tears began to flow down her cheeks. She thanked us for stopping and being there for her. I told her that we started praying a long time ago for people we would meet along this journey, and she was an answer to our prayers.

Lloyd invited her and her children to join us for dinner at our campground. We were staying just down the road a couple miles from where she was. Unfortunately, she was not able to be there, but I continue to pray that she is finding that love and healing in her heart that only Jesus can bring.

Our Only Hope

Maybe you are reading this and need that love, forgiveness and healing in your life. So many have been hurt by others in relationships and need healing. Don't look any further than Jesus. He is your answer. Turn to Him, seek Him. It doesn't take much searching, because the minute you turn around, He is right there waiting for you with open arms.

Here is a little bit of that story of the prodigal son I mentioned earlier. Watch what happened when the son decides to turn back and come home.

> *But when he came to himself, he said, 'How many of my father's hired servants have bread enough and to spare, and I perish with hunger!*
>
> *I will arise and go to my father, and will say to him, "Father, I have sinned against heaven and before you,*
>
> *and I am no longer worthy to be called your son. Make me like one of your hired servants." '*
>
> *And he arose and came to his father. But when he was still a great way off, his father saw him and had compassion, and ran and fell on his neck and kissed him.*
>
> *And the son said to him, 'Father, I have sinned against heaven and in your sight, and am no longer worthy to be called your son.'*
>
> *But the father said to his servants, 'Bring out the best robe and put it on him, and put a ring on his hand and sandals on his feet.*
>
> *And bring the fatted calf here and kill it, and let us eat and be merry;*
>
> *for this my son was dead and is alive again; he was lost and is found.' And they began to be merry.* -**Luke 15:17-24**

There was no judgment on the Father's part, no "*I told you so*" attitude; only joy, love and forgiveness. The Father knew that the son was repentant and sorry, so there was no need to re-hash the past.

The past was now past. He was forgiven and the rejoicing had begun because he was lost, but now was found. What a story, what a day!

What a day it was for us as well! I'll admit, they aren't all like today. It's like fishing, some days you catch fish, some days you don't. But you'll never catch fish without casting out your line. We're called to be *"fishers of men."* Today was a good day to catch fish. We thanked the Lord for drawing hearts to Him today and saving their souls. We are only planting and watering, and your Word reminds us *"You bring the growth."* (1 Corinthians 3:6)

The riding went well today, but with the city riding and hills we climbed, we only managed a very long and arduous 75 miles or so. One thing that Zjelko shared with me on the bike today really spoke to me. He has been saying something for years and years, not really knowing what it meant or how it might happen. But the Lord knew. *"California here we come!"* Yes, Zjelko, *"California here we come!"*

Day 7 – September 12th

On the bike today by 7:30am and by day's end we hammered out another 86 miles. Along the way we found a rare tail wind for part of the day which made for some nice riding. However, we also faced some steep hills.

After speaking to one man, he reminded us that now we were in the Bible Belt. One thing we did realize was that many of the people we would talk with would say they were believers. As I began to think of this, it made me wonder how many people who call themselves believers are truly *"followers"* of Christ.

One of main reasons for *"Mission 66"* is to call those in the church back to Christ. This may sound odd because we equate *going to church* with being a *Christian*. Now, going to church should be a part of our Christian walk, but we must be sure that when we walk out of the church on Sunday morning that we are living like the church the other six days. This question that we ask, *"Do you go to church?"* is not a correct statement if we believe that *the church* is God's people and not a building.

Our Only Hope

We are to *"be the church"* not *"go to church."* What happens on Sunday morning should be an overflow of worship from our hearts as we gather together to express and give thanks to the Lord for all that He means to us. But the enemy has convinced so many to *"go to church"* rather than *"be the church."* It's easy to say you're a Christian because you go to church. It's quite another thing to surrender your life to Jesus Christ and count the cost before we decide to follow Him.

Back in 2004, our family, with 14 other families, planted a church which I currently pastor. To get a feel for our community, I made survey cards for our core team to ask people questions about what they liked or disliked about church. As I mentioned a few pages back, the two most common answers to the question of what they didn't like about church were:

1) **They just want your money**

2) **They're just a bunch of hypocrites**

If we say were believers of Christ, we must be sure we're following Him. Because if we only *"talk the talk"* and don't *"walk the walk,"* we're giving Christ a bad name. People are looking for every opportunity to call us a bunch of hypocrites.

I heard an evangelist say once, *"If you aren't living like a follower of Christ, don't tell others you're a Christian, instead tell them you are a satan worshipper. Give satan a bad name, not Jesus."* Hmm...makes you think, huh? But if the world would truly see us living out our faith and not simply *"going to church"* on Sunday morning, they would take notice and know where to turn when they have questions about life.

James reminds us to:

> **be doers of the word and not hearers only, deceiving yourselves. -James 1:22**

It takes more than just believing, because later in his small yet powerful book, James writes...

> **Even the demons believe – and tremble! -James 2:19**

We must make a point to truly live what we say we believe and afford others the opportunity to recognize that the power of the Holy Spirit does truly dwell within us. *"Mission 66...If My People"* is calling God's people back to Biblical values so that the light of Christ begins to shine once again in this dark world. Only those who know Christ can be His light. So, let's make a point to *"be the church,"* and not just *"go to church."*

One man I came across as we were flying down this huge hill into a small town, was sitting alone outside his home. As we talked, I found that he attended the church building right next to his home. It was only a stone's throw away. However, I could sense from some of the remnants of his habits near him, that he was struggling to live out what he said he believed in.

I did offer to pray with him to re-dedicate his life to Christ, which he agreed to do. But you see, I believe he was deceived into thinking that the church building was his salvation, rather than the cleansing blood of Jesus Christ who paid for our sin on the cross so that we could live a victorious life! I pray that the Holy Spirit takes hold of his heart and he begins to make changes in his life. I pray also that the Holy Spirit continues to take hold of my heart and make changes in my life till the day I die. None of us will ever *"arrive"* until we see Jesus face to face. But in the meantime, let's begin to walk in His righteousness and not our own sinfulness or self-righteousness. Christ came to set us free…let's believe it and begin to live like it.

We spent the night at an RV Park at Glen Oaks called, *"Lamplight Lane RV Resort."* The owners of the park, John and Barbara, are followers of Christ and were such a blessing to us during our very short stay. Once they heard about the *"Mission 66"* vision, they blessed our team with $100 for trip expenses along the way. As I thought about the people who have blessed us in so many different ways, I thought of the verse found in Proverbs 11:25…

> *The generous soul will be made rich, And he who waters will also be watered himself.*

It's true! As we refresh others, the Bible reminds us that we will also be refreshed. Lord, thank you for refreshing us through this wonderful couple today. I know that they will be refreshed in their lives for their obedience to You. Who might the Lord be speaking to your heart to go and refresh today? Let's look for those opportunities as we walk through our days.

Day 8 – September 13th

Three years ago today, God began to stir this vision in my heart. At the time, I had no idea who would be a part of this team. It was simply a thought, a seed in my heart that you placed there. But that seed took root, was watered and began to grow. The team we have, as you read in the introduction, is such a varied group of people from so many walks of life. The one thing that I believe a team of any sort needs to be successful and accomplish their goal is unity.

Take for instance a sports team. You could have a team with less talent, but unified, outplay a more experienced and talented team which is selfish and disunified. Check out the beginning and end of Psalm 133 and what comes to those who live together in unity.

> *...how good and how pleasant it is for brethren to dwell together in unity! For there the Lord commanded the blessing – Life forevermore. -Psalm 133:1, 3*

Without unity, there is no blessing. With unity, He commands His blessing!

In marriage, in relationships, in the workplace, amongst followers of Christ; to accomplish anything with meaning and purpose there must be unity.

Today the team had opportunities to pass out many of the Mission 66 tracts along the way. Lloyd, who left on his bike around 4am, had a chance to pray with a young lady at a convenience store to accept the Lord. We would end our day in Springfield at the General Council of the Assemblies of God.

What a wonderful opportunity to meet with Dr. George Wood, our Superintendent, and Dr. James Bradford. It was great to receive a

St. Louis, Missouri

tour of the building and hear the history of the Assemblies of God. What a wonderful fellowship we're a part of. What a blessing to stay in the Central Assembly of God parking lot with our camper while others were shuttled to a friend's house that now lives in this area. Pat Sullivan and his family were so kind to our team and even hosted some of them in their home and provided food, warm showers and even Krispy Kreme donuts in the morning!

Lloyd and Brian went to a truck stop to try and get some warm showers and experienced a powerful testimony in one guy's life. In Lloyd's words...

As we went to the "Flying J" truck stop, I asked and we got the shower for free. Brian was laughing. The guy who opened the shower for Brian then went outside for a smoke. As I walked by him, he seemed upset so I asked him, "Are you okay?"

He began to open up to me and share how his girlfriend had cheated on him and he was thinking there was nothing left to live for. As we talked, I found that he had a child and nephew who he was close to and encouraged him to live for them. He shared how as a young man he had experienced very devastating situations and that his life was one big mess of alcohol and drugs with no hope.

I shared Jesus with him and when Brian came out, we prayed together with him. After we prayed, he threw his arms around my neck and wept for a long time. He appreciated the time we spent listening and praying for him.

I don't believe that he became a Christian at that moment, but certainly some good seed was planted.

It's such a blessing to continue to see the Lord directing our steps this entire trip.

One moment today had Brian and I laughing, unfortunately at Joel's expense! We stopped at a huge variety store and parked our bikes out front. After looking around, we came back out and Joel looked one way for his bike and didn't see it. Thinking his bike was stolen, he shouted, "*Where's my bike?*" I think for a few seconds his blood pressure shot up and his pulse skyrocketed when he thought he

Our Only Hope

lost his bike. Meanwhile, his bike was parked right next to mine and Brian's. We laughed so hard because Joel is super calm and it was unusual for him to get this excited!

Have you ever lost something? A wallet, your keys, a car? I read a story of a man in Germany who exited a store and couldn't find his car in the parking lot. He reported it stolen, but in reality he just forgot where he parked it because twenty years later (yes, you read that correctly) they found it!

Luke writes in his Gospel about things that were lost. A lost sheep, a lost coin and a lost son. Parables are short stories that Jesus used to teach or explain a spiritual truth. We already looked at the lost prodigal son, now let's take a closer look at the other two lost items found in the same chapter of Luke 15.

Parable of the Lost Sheep

What man of you, having a hundred sheep, if he loses one of them, does not leave the ninety-nine in the wilderness, and go after the one which is lost until he finds it? And when he has found it, he lays it on his shoulders, rejoicing. And when he comes home, he calls together his friends and neighbors, saying to them, 'Rejoice with me, for I have found my sheep which was lost!' I say to you that likewise there will be more joy in heaven over one sinner who repents than over ninety-nine just persons who need no repentance.

Parable of the Lost Coin

Or what woman, having ten silver coins, if she loses one coin, does not light a lamp, sweep the house, and search carefully until she finds it? And when she has found it, she calls her friends and neighbors together, saying, 'Rejoice with me, for I have found the piece which I lost!' Likewise, I say to you, there is joy in the presence of the angels of God over one sinner who repents.

Each of these stories has the similarity that something was lost, searched for and found. One other commonality is the comparison to one sinner who repents and the great rejoicing that takes place in the presence God. Have you ever truly thought about the day you came to accept Christ in your life, that angels in heaven actually rejoiced before God? Can you imagine that scene, just for you? It reminds me of the line we sing to the song Amazing Grace that says, *"I once was lost but now I'm found."* It's like when the lost son was found at the end of this same chapter and the Father is explaining to the other son why they were rejoicing. He said,

> **It was right that we should make merry and be glad, for your brother was dead and is alive again, and was lost and is found. Luke 15:32**

Maybe you're still lost. Maybe today is the day you'll be found. The thing is, the Lord already knows where you're at. It's not like hide and seek, that He has to look for you.

Do you remember when Adam and Eve were hiding in the Garden of Eden and God asked the question, *"Where are you?"* Actually, this is the very first question God asks in the Bible. But it was not referring to where they were physically, He was actually asking where they were spiritually. They were lost and hiding from God because of the sin that had entered their world. We were born into this sinful world with a sinful nature. Therefore, until we ask Christ to forgive us and be our Savior, we're lost and in hiding as well. But today, you can be found. And if you are, just know there is a great big celebration going on in heaven…just for you!

So, where are you?

Day 9 – September 14th

Go therefore and make disciples of all the nations…
-Matthew 28:19

Our Only Hope

Today it hit me as I handed a Mission 66 tract to a family from England. We could literally reach the world from this road! Yesterday we met a family from Italy and who knows who we will meet tomorrow? I believe the Lord brings people into our path that He wants us to be a light to every day. Whether we are on a famous road in America, a vacation overseas, a business trip, or a busy mom at a soccer game…the people before us are our mission field.

Today heated up quickly. The 90 miles we completed on the bike would match the temperature today. While waiting for Ralph to pick us up from our stopping point and shuttle us to where we would spend the night, another divine appointment walked into our path. God's timing is always perfect. If Ralph would've arrived a few minutes earlier or we would've biked a little further, we would have missed what happened next.

A lady came walking towards me and asked if I had a couple of dollars for gas. I walked over to the car with her where she and Ben were trying to scrounge up what change they had to put in their tank. As I gave them some money, I spoke to them about what Christ did for all of us. They were appreciative of the help and they took time to pray a simple prayer to re-dedicate their lives to Christ. I handed them one of the Gospels of John and encouraged them to be in the Word of God consistently.

We met many people today. Randy, Micah and Squirrel to name a few. Squirrel was the most interesting one I met. When I asked him why his name was *"Squirrel,"* he answered, *"Because I'm squirrely."* Ask a dumb question, get a logical response, right? We had a chance to pray with some today as we encountered many believers along Rte. 66.

One man today stood out to me by what he said and got me thinking about my life. Randy made the comment, *"I'm simply taking life day by day."* I know sometimes I can worry so much about the future that I forget to live in the moment. If I'm not careful, I can miss so much of what the Lord has for me today, because I'm rushing around worrying or just thinking about tomorrow.

> *Therefore, I say to you, do not worry about your life, what you will eat or what you will drink; nor about your body, what you will put on. Is not life more than food and the body more than clothing?*
>
> *Look at the birds of the air, for they neither sow nor reap nor gather into barns; yet your heavenly Father feeds them. Are you not of more value than they?*
>
> *Which of you by worrying can add one cubit to his stature?*
>
> *So why do you worry about clothing? Consider the lilies of the field, how they grow: they neither toil nor spin; and yet I say to you that even Solomon in all his glory was not arrayed like one of these.*
>
> *Now if God so clothes the grass of the field, which today is, and tomorrow is thrown into the oven, will He not much more clothe you, O you of little faith?*
>
> *Therefore do not worry, saying 'What shall we eat?' or 'What shall we wear?' For after all these things the Gentiles seek. For your heavenly Father knows that you need all these things. But seek first the kingdom of God and His righteousness, and all these things shall be added unto you. Therefore do not worry about tomorrow, for tomorrow will worry about its own things. Sufficient for the day is its own trouble. -Matthew 6:25-34*

Wow, those are some powerful words Jesus spoke! Now combine those with the words that Jesus' half-brother wrote.

> *Come now, you who say, "Today or tomorrow we will go to such and such a city, spend a year there, buy and sell, and make a profit"; whereas you do not know what will happen tomorrow. For what is your life? It is even a vapor that appears for a little time and then vanishes away. Instead you ought to say, "If the Lord wills, we shall live and do this or that." But now you boast in your arrogance. All such boasting is evil. Therefore, to him who knows to do good and does not do it, to him it is sin. -James 4:13-17*

Our Only Hope

These two places in Scripture remind us to live for today and not get too far ahead of ourselves. That doesn't mean we don't plan for tomorrow. What it means is that we don't worry about tomorrow, because if we worry about tomorrow we will rob ourselves and deny God the opportunity to work in our lives today. May we strive to live like Randy reminded me today, *"one day at a time."*

This is the day the Lord has made, We will rejoice and be glad in it. -Psalm 118:24

It's a choice to rejoice. But it's hard to rejoice in today when we're always thinking or worrying about tomorrow.

St. Louis, Missouri

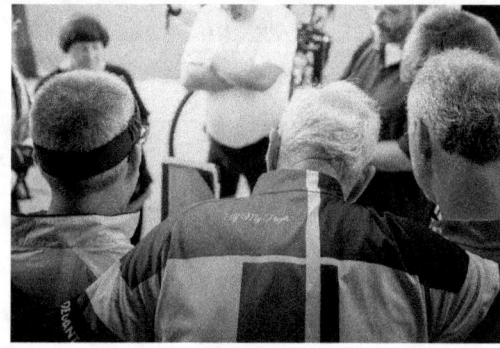

CHAPTER 5
KANSAS TO OKLAHOMA

 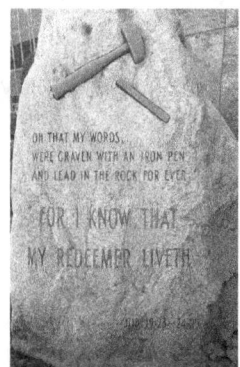 

Day 10 – September 15th

Today was such a long day! The winds, as was common on this trip, were hitting us from the side or directly in our faces all day. 86 miles later, we landed in Chelsea, Oklahoma.

The day started early for one of our team members, Lloyd, who decided to get a head start on the day and bike out while it was still dark around 4:30am. As he was riding before the sun came up, a pick-up truck came within inches of taking him out and ripped the mirror right off his handlebar. Joel & Zeljko also had a close call as a car was riding the white line and they could feel the breeze of the car on their shoulders.

One thing we do as we begin our day and before we head out on the roads is pray. Today especially, we were grateful for His covering and protection over our team on the bikes. An inch or two here or there and this day could've ended up a whole lot different. No matter if we are biking or simply leaving our house each day, prayer should never be neglected because it truly invites His presence to cover our lives.

> *The Lord is my rock and my fortress and my deliverer; My God, my strength, in whom I will trust; My shield and the horn of my salvation, my stronghold. -Psalm 18:2*
>
> *He shall cover you with His feathers, And under His wings you shall take refuge; His truth shall be your shield and buckler. -Psalm 91:4*
>
> *You are my hiding place and my shield; I hope in Your word. -Psalm 119:114*

The only way to recognize His presence over our lives is to grow closer to Him each new day.

Lloyd had a wonderful opportunity to share Christ with two ladies in a Walmart early this morning. As he showed them one of the videos that Austin worked on, they both began to cry when they heard Christ being shared. At that point, Lloyd simply asked if they needed to get right with the Lord. They said they were just talking about that before he approached them. Lloyd then had an incredible opportunity to pray with them to re-dedicate their lives to Christ.

Later in the day we met a lady in a McDonald's who really touched my heart. You can tell that she did not have much of this world's possessions, but she was a follower and believer of Christ. After talking and praying with her, she reached in her pocket and gave me two dollars toward our trip. It reminded me of the story of the poor widow in Mark 12:41-44.

> *Now Jesus sat opposite the treasury and saw how the people put money into the treasury. And many who were rich put in much. Then one poor widow came and threw in two mites, which make a quadrans. So He called His disciples to Himself and said to them, "Assuredly, I say to you that this poor widow has put in more than all those who have given to the treasury; for they all put in out of their abundance, but she out of her poverty put in all that she had, her whole livelihood".*

That last part gets me… *"her whole livelihood."* Imagine that! Taking every last cent you have to your name with you to church on Sunday and putting it in the offering plate!

As this lady handed me those two dollars, it made a statement that she was ALL IN. Money says so much about our character and determines so much about where we're building our kingdom - in heaven or here on earth. This lady's two bucks would only buy us a drink or two, not much when you look at the big picture of our expenses. But to her it really wasn't about the amount, it was more about being obedient to give what she had to accomplish the Lord's work and was an especially rich blessing to us. How we handle money says a lot about our priorities in life.

On another note, something I would like to know when I get to heaven is how a seventy-nine year old man is physically able to bike with this team. We often say about Zeljko… *"He can hardly walk… but he sure can ride a bike."* And his wife, Hilda, is a gem!

Because of our limited sleeping arrangements, there are many nights that their support vehicle during the day turns into their sleeping quarters at night. Everything is pulled out from the back, the seats fold down and they put their mattress on the floor. It's simply amazing to watch our eldest couple hang right in there with this crew. Today as we rode, Zeljko said to me, *"This is a new season in my life."*

I must be honest, at his age, I was thinking, "A *new season?!*" But the verse in Psalm 92:14 reminds us that **"they shall bear fruit in** *their old age; they shall be fresh and flourishing."* Zeljko and his wonderful wife Hilda are living testimonies of this verse.

As we pedaled side by side, Zeljko began to quote verses from the book of Ecclesiastes, chapter 3 verse 1, which begins like this.

> ***To everything there is a season, A time for every purpose under heaven.***

This chapter truly is a beautiful piece of poetry that Solomon wrote. We're all in different seasons in our lives. As I am writing this chapter today, I'm on a plane leaving a dear friend of mine in Sweden, and the verses I just wrote are his favorite verses in the Bible. I read it with him before leaving his home early this morning. And as I sit and write this part of the book and fly over the tip of Greenland towards my home back in the states, I can't help but ask myself the question, *"What season of life am I in?"*

Seasons come, and seasons go. Some are fun, some are boring, some are difficult, some seem to last forever. But no matter what season we are in, remember, there might be a new one straight ahead. This one won't last forever. And the season you may find yourself in right now is always for a purpose.

Kunal, my friend in Sweden, said something to me on the way to the airport this morning that I agree with. He said, *"I stopped believing in coincidences a long time ago. Everything happens for a reason."* The season that he finds himself in right now is one of those difficult seasons.

Zjelko finds himself in an exciting season as his years wind down, even though you wouldn't know they are winding down. May the seasons we find ourselves in begin to shape who we are as we allow them to take their course and as the flowers begin to bloom or the leaves begin to fall. Sure, we would all like to be in the season of *"dancing, gathering stones, or love."* But that's not how life is all the time. Those seasons come, but so do times of *"casting away, mourning and weeping."* It's just a part of the fallen world we live in.

Don't get stuck in your seasons of life. Allow them to come and go as you pass through them and remember above all to keep your focus on Christ and stay continually in His Word. He will bring you through it.

> ***And we know that God works all things together for good, for those who love God and are called according to His purpose. -Romans 8:28***

This verse is available for everyone, but everyone doesn't receive the benefits of it until they love God. Until someone comes to know Christ, they can't say that *"all things work together for good."* But once you know Him in your life, as hard as it may be at times, you can declare this through the most difficult seasons in your life.

The seasons that are most challenging are the ones we need to praise Him the most. It's easy to praise Him when we go through the fun, easy seasons of life. But it's those dry, hard seasons that seem to last the longest, hurt the most and make it difficult to praise Him. But it's these seasons that shape and develop our character the most. But how we go through them will determine how we're shaped when we come out on the other side.

I find it true that these difficult seasons seem to last longer than the lighter seasons in life. Much like the seasons that come and go in central Pennsylvania. I love summer, even spring and fall are great… not so much winter. All these seasons last around three months give or take, but guess which one seems to go on forever? I'll give you four guesses and the first three don't count. It's those long, dark, cold nights of winter that seem to last longer than the warm, stay up late nights of summer. But each season eventually comes to an end as a new one begins.

If you find yourself in a difficult season, don't give up, don't quit. Keep pressing through, **"being confident of this very thing, that He who has begun a good work in you will complete it until the day of Jesus Christ."** (***Philippians 1:6***). The prophet Isaiah also reminds us that the Lord will never leave us in the middle of our difficult seasons.

Our Only Hope

Fear not, for I have redeemed you; I have called you by your name; You are Mine. When you pass through the waters, I will be with you;

And through the rivers, they shall not overflow you;

When you walk through the fire, you shall not be burned, Nor shall the flame scorch you. -Isaiah 43:1, 2

Did you see it? He's taking you through the season. He will not abandon you or leave you in the middle of it. Press into the Lord, He's got you! A new season is on the horizon.

As we biked through a small town, we had a great opportunity to bike down a road that led to the house where Mickey Mantle grew up.

"The Mick" played his entire Major League career with the New York Yankees from 1951-1968. Remember when players stayed with teams their entire career? He died just shy of his 64th birthday on August 13, 1995. His son, Billy, died of heart failure in March of 1994 after being treated for Hodgkin's disease, which was the same illness that claimed his father and grandfather.

We stood on the stoop of his front porch where a plaque honors his home and the father who raised him.

What humble beginnings for a great ball player. What I learned today on his front porch was that his baseball skills developed because of a father who took time and would go out in the yard with his son and toss the ball around and teach him how to hit. His dad took time.

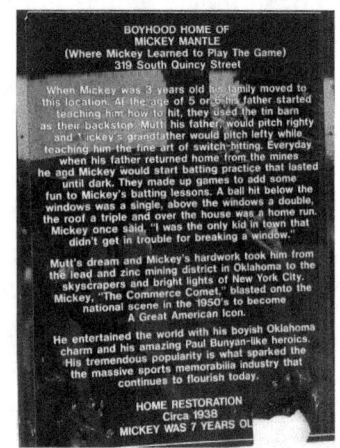

We are living in a day and age where fathers are becoming less and less involved with their children. The days of playing ball in the yard with our kids is diminishing.

Dads, take every moment you can to spend time with your kids. Both moms and dads play such vital roles in the life of their children. Each have such wonderful qualities to offer their children. Unfortunately, there are so many single moms raising their children by themselves. Dads, may I encourage you to be there for your children. They need time with both mom and dad.

Help them with their homework. Teach them about integrity, honesty, and how to manage money. Most importantly, be an example of what it looks like to follow Christ. They need to see that example in you. Dads, you play a vital role not only in the lives of your children, but how that ultimately impacts our communities and land that we live in. Look at the very last verse of the Old Testament.

> ***And he will turn the hearts of the fathers to the children, And the hearts of the children to their fathers, Lest I come and strike the land with a curse. -Malachi 4:6***

Do you mean that our land could be under a curse because the hearts of the fathers are not turned to their children? That's powerful. Could that mean that our land can be healed if dads would begin to turn their hearts to their children once again? I believe so.

Dads, let's be the fathers we were called to be. We have great responsibility in this position the Lord has placed us in. Mickey Mantle's dad gave his son something that is more precious than anything. A glove, a bat, a ball? No, he gave his time. You see, through time you can teach anything. Take time with your kids, Dad, you'll never regret it. It's never too late to begin a new season and turn your hearts to your children. Now - that is one season that should never end!

The end of the day was a test on my body. I literally did not know if I would be able to finish the day. Most of the team was pretty far ahead of me and I found myself alone for the last stretch of the day. The heat was getting to me and I was hungry, and the winds in my face weren't helping much. I called my daughter, son, wife and a good friend to pray for me. I'm very grateful for the power we find in prayer and the support of family and friends.

> *Call upon Me in the day of trouble; I will deliver you, and you shall glorify Me. -Psalm 50:15*

What a blessing it was to feel the Lord give me strength to finish the day. Today's over and tomorrow will be here before we know it. Time to get some rest.

Day 11 – September 16th

Having seen the forecast for the day, an early start on the bikes was in order. That is easier said than done when you have so many trying to get ready at the same time. The winds would grow stronger as the day grew longer, and the temperatures would reach into the nineties. Today would be one of our lowest days of pedaling, about 50 miles. But it's how we ended the day that made it quite unique.

Lloyd met a man, Larry, in the small town of Galena, Kansas. Old Route 66 just skirts this state for a few miles. Dalton's de-railer broke, so we stopped at the top of a hill under a shade tree to rest and waited for the support team to show up with supplies and lunch. When they arrived, so did Lloyd riding in Larry's SUV.

We enjoyed lunch under the tree where we then had the privilege of meeting Jimmie. He was a part of the Christian camp ground beside where we decided to stop and have lunch. We had no idea that this was a Christian camp or that we would meet these guys along the way today. But that is part of the excitement of the journey, how the Lord brings people across our path at just the right time.

Jimmie shared with us about a ministry he began called *"Salvage Life Restorations."* He teaches by using the analogy of restoring *"old jalopies"* and turning them into something new, and how the Lord wants to transform our lives as well. In Jimmie's words: *"You Can Recover, You Are Worth Fixing, and You Can Smile Again."*

Larry then treated us as he helped shuttle our team to a Car Museum in town. If you like old cars, you've got to see this place. I'm not a car guy, but even I thought it was pretty cool.

After enjoying a break from the bikes, Larry offered to help shuttle our team to our next destination point in Stroud, Oklahoma. Being a Saturday, we would put down temporary roots here for two nights rather than our typical one night. Pastor Jeremy and Angie would welcome us warmly into the town and the congregation of Stroud First Assembly was so kind as we rested and were refreshed for two nights.

We settled in with a pulled pork dinner and they even projected the movie "*Cars*" onto the wall of the fellowship hall for the team to enjoy, popcorn and all. I still have to see the movie as my evenings were pretty full with details to go over from the current day and preparing for the next one.

The day did not go anywhere near as I had planned, but I believe the Lord fully intended for us to rest a little bit more today and enjoy fellowship with new friends. The day did provide some great ministry opportunities as a lady at a bus stop in Tulsa, Oklahoma re-dedicated her life to Christ and we prayed for another lady named Cindy for emotional and financial security in her life.

A person that really stood out during the time on the roads today was a man who was working at a convenience store. He had just arrived in America 10 days ago. He was from Pakistan. As I shared the Gospel with him, he seemed very eager to learn more. The way he responded and the questions he asked made me think this may have been the very first time he ever heard about Jesus. He had never heard of a Savior that loves him and died to save him from his sins.

One thing we all know about ourselves is that we have *"all have sinned and fall short of the glory of God." (Romans 3:23).* I trust that this man also comes to realize that *"the wages of sin is death, but the gift of God is eternal life in Christ Jesus our Lord." (Romans 6:23).* He gladly received the Gospel of John and I know that it says His Word *"shall not return to Me void, but it shall accomplish what I please, and it shall prosper in the thing for which I sent it." Isaiah 55:11.*

My prayer is that the Lord would accomplish in this man's heart what only He can do.

Day 12 – September 17th

Sundays! Worship, fellowship and rest. Doesn't get much better than this. Except when I get to preach as well. This morning Pastor Jeremy asked if I would share the message, *"Our Only Hope"* with his congregation. One lady, Chrystal, who was visiting from out of town, came forward to re-dedicate her life to Christ. It was also a huge blessing to see Jimmie, the man we met yesterday, drive down to be with us in worship this morning.

Following service, we were treated to lunch at the *"Rock Café."* O.K., so Sunday did just get better.

This restaurant became famous because of two things. One, in the movie *"Cars,"* the character, *"Sally"* (Porsche 911) was inspired by Dawn at the *"Rock Café."*

Secondly, this café has also been a featured restaurant on the show *"Diners, Drive-ins and Dives."* I had to get what they made on that show, the *"Bison Burger."* Let's just say that after tasting their food, they truly deserved an appearance on the show.

Later that afternoon, Joel and I decided to walk around town and met one of the pastors from the Methodist church. What a great meeting we enjoyed with this brother on the streets of Stroud, Oklahoma. Most of the afternoon was spent resting, journaling and relaxing. Unless you were Brian and Lloyd who found a race car track and test drove some crazy fast cars. I must say, these two love to have fun and definitely don't let any grass grow under their feet. For them to sit and rest, may be, well… torture!

They came back with quite the stories of driving these cars around the track they found…somehow, someway. That's one thing I've noticed with Lloyd, if there's a will there's a way. I was just glad they came back in one piece. And I was super glad that everyone, especially Brian and Lloyd, signed their waiver forms for this trip.

In the evening, the church had a praise, prayer and testimony night. Dalton assisted the youth pastor in leading worship and it was a powerful time to pray and hear from the Lord. The congregation made us feel so at home as we all mingled around following the service and shared a meal together. I must say it was hard to leave Stroud—Pastor Jeroyme and Stroud First Assembly, thank you! You've blessed us in a countless number of ways. What great new friends we are meeting along Rte. 66. Two Sundays down, three to go. It's been a great weekend, what will tomorrow hold?

Day 13 - Monday, September 18th

Well, we all know that Mondays can be hard. This day welcomed us with a strong, steady rainfall. The rain caused where we parked the trailer two days ago to get stuck in the mud. As Ralph improvised, we prayed.

I've never seen a trailer pulled the way Ralph decided to try it! I must hand it to him, he is creative in his thinking. Not only did we pray, but others back home were contacted and began praying as well. We were in a very precarious situation. Because of the mud, Ralph couldn't hook up his truck and pull the trailer through the normal way, so he used some ropes and attached his truck and hitch to the opposite end of the camper. Don't ask me how, only by prayer, but he got that trailer moved without incident.

The heavy rains caused some of us to ride a few miles in the support vehicle, while some of the others braved the elements. Later that day, I hurt my shoulder which would prevent me from finishing the day and one of the other riders, Brian, hurt his wrist. Then, as Ralph and Sherie arrived at the house we were staying at, upon backing up into the driveway, they skimmed the edge of the roof

Our Only Hope

which damaged both the trailer and the roof line, gutter and shingles. Let's just say, it was not the best start to the week!

But I love how the Lord knows what you are going through and can place on other people's hearts Scripture verses and things to pray for you at just the right time. A dear friend, Diane, from our congregation back home texted us the following thoughts even before this day began to unravel.

"Feel very strongly on this today. Please take Isaiah 54:17 with you all as well today. NO weapon(s) will prosper against this team. Fine tune into the voice of the Holy Spirit."

Can you see how the Lord impressed upon Diane's heart the need to pray and give us this Word from the Lord…for today? Here is that verse in its entirety. Maybe you need it in your life right now, or maybe tomorrow…or next Monday when your camper gets stuck in some awful mud!

> **No weapon formed against you shall prosper, And every tongue which rises against you in judgment You shall condemn. This is the heritage of the servants of the Lord, And their righteousness is from Me," Says the Lord.**
> **-Isaiah 54:17**

This verse proved itself over and over again today as we faced one hurdle, or weapon, after another. The weather, the mud, the trailer, the injuries. Even my shoulder injury came about in a peculiar manner.

It happened as I was stretching around to reach into the back pocket of my bike jersey to pull out a gospel of John to give to a man named Fred who had just given his life to Christ. The thrill of seeing Fred make a choice to follow Christ made me not think much about my shoulder, until I hopped back on my bike. It was my right shoulder, but I literally could not use my hand to shift the gears without a shooting pain up to my shoulder. As I was disappointed not to finish the ride today, my son, Luke, reminded me on the phone that night that this trip *"wasn't about getting from point A to point B, but rather it was about the people we were to meet."*

When we arrived at the house of Bill and Sue Smith, Ralph and Sherie shared with me about the damage to the house and camper. I'll tell you, the enemy was trying hard with his weapons today, but I love the verse in 1 John 4:4 that reminds us that *"He (Christ) who is in you is greater than he (satan) who is in the world."* And then I think about what Diane told us just that morning, *"no weapon(s) will prosper against this team."* I trust that this encourages you to share with people any verses that the Lord places on your heart for them. I know for us today, it made all the difference for our team.

I must say that of all the team members, Ralph and Sherie have sacrificed so much and have their work cut out for them each and every day. We may be pedaling miles on a bike, but the tasks they have before them each day is grueling. Ralph and Sherie, thank you for giving so much to make this missions trip possible. May the Lord bless you for your faithfulness and reward you someday for your obedience to respond to His calling on Mission 66.

As we ended this day, I wrote these words in my journal.

"I trust You, Lord, that as long as You want me to not bike, that You have people in mind for me to meet that I would not have otherwise met had I been on the bike. Show me Your will for the days ahead…and I thank You for Your healing in Your perfect will, way and timing."

Day 14 - Tuesday, September 19th

Bill and Sue have been amazing hosts on our quick, overnight stay. Last night they ordered out and we enjoyed a wonderful Mexican fajita buffet and this morning they had the coffee brewing early and a breakfast ready to go to help us get our day started off on the right foot. We joined together in prayer and I'll never forget Sue praying specifically for healing in my shoulder and then Bill prayed for Brian's wrist. The visit with the Smiths was just what we needed after a very difficult previous day. The pool and hot tub outside also helped soothe our aches and pains.

Today would be challenging for me because I've never had to sit out an entire day of riding; either on the last coast to coast trip or this one. But I know the Lord was in this because today would be my

Our Only Hope

good friend's first riding day with our team. Gary arrived in from the Pittsburgh area yesterday afternoon and his timing could not have been more perfect. As much as I would have liked to ride today with my friend, Gary stepped in and took my place. To accomplish a mission like this, it truly takes a team. Not only a team of riders, but a support team and a host of people along Rt. 66 that continue to help along the way.

Today I was reflecting on the timing of things on this trip. It made me stop and think about the timing of Christ coming to earth. The Apostle Paul writes in **Galatians 4:4**...

> ***But when the fullness of the time had come, God sent forth His Son, born of a woman, born under the law, to redeem those who were under the law, that we might receive the adoption as sons.***

And when he speaks of perfect timing, Paul states it so well in **Romans 5:6**...

> ***For when we were still without strength, in due time Christ died for the ungodly.***

Christ came to earth, at just the right time, and took our place on the cross as payment for our sins. What was due to us He took upon Himself. What mercy! Jesus received what we deserved. Grace is just the opposite, when we receive what we don't deserve. His forgiveness, His love and eternal life.

What a thought when you stop to think of exactly what Christ did. He left His Father's side - for *us*. He left heaven, to come to earth, for *us*. While we were yet sinners, Paul writes a little later in Romans 5, Jesus Christ hung on the cross...for *us*. No one else ever did that and no one else ever will. Jesus, thank you for taking our place at just the right time, while we were in our mess and literally your enemy, You came and You died...for *us*.

I'm so glad Gary showed up to join the team. His timing was perfect! Today proved to be the hardest and most strenuous day of biking thus far. Gary may not have appreciated his first day of riding

Kansas to Oklahoma

as much as he anticipated. Strong head winds would hammer them all day long! OK, maybe it wasn't such a bad day to be off the bike after all. The team also met up with a guy, Mike, who was biking across the country. His dad was following close behind him in his car. As far as my shoulder goes, I'm trusting the Lord will put me back on the bike…in His perfect timing.

Day 15 - Wednesday, September 20th

Even though my shoulder was still tender, as I awoke, I knew that many were praying and I recalled Sue's powerful prayer for healing the night before. I decided to take a step of faith and ride. So much power flows from what He accomplished for us on the cross. His blood that was shed first and foremost for the forgiveness of our sins has also provided for divine healing in our bodies. Hundreds of years before Christ accomplished His work on the cross, Isaiah prophesied…

> *Surely He has borne our griefs And carried our sorrows;*
>
> *Yet we esteemed Him stricken, Smitten by God, and afflicted.*
>
> *But He was wounded for our transgressions, He was bruised for our iniquities;*
>
> *The chastisement for our peace was upon Him, And by His stripes we are healed.   -Isaiah 53:4, 5*

Forgiveness, healing, peace…what promises!

The Psalmist David puts it this way.

> *Bless the Lord, O my soul, And forget not all His benefits:*
>
> *Who forgives all your iniquities, Who heals all your diseases,*
>
> *Who redeems your life from destruction, Who crowns you with lovingkindness and tender mercies,*
>
> *Who satisfies your mouth with good things, So that your youth if renewed like the eagle's.   -Psalm 103:2-5*

What a testimony today as I re-joined the team and rode 85 miles without one twinge of pain in my shoulder! Come to think of it, I don't think I've felt this strong the entire trip. To go from not being able to shift gears two days ago, not riding yesterday, to no pain at all today. This could only be attributed to the power of prayer and the Lord's healing. I believe the Lord also knew my desire to be back on the bike today. It reminded me of a verse from Psalm 37:4 that Joel and I were talking about as we rode together. It says,

Delight yourself also in the Lord, and He shall give you the desires of your heart.

It's so true. Of course we want the desires of our heart, but first we must learn to place priority on delighting ourselves in the Lord. Many verses can be pulled out of context if not used in their entirety.

Here are a couple of examples.

Therefore submit to God. Resist the devil and he will flee from you. -James 4:7

If we don't do the first part of this verse, the second part is impossible. How many people are walking around trying to resist the devil and he isn't fleeing? Why? Because their lives aren't submitted to God. However, when our lives are submitted to God, we can resist the devil all day long and he must flee from us. He has no choice.

How about this verse?

There is therefore now no condemnation to those who are in Christ Jesus, who do not walk according to the flesh, but according to the Spirit. -Romans 8:1

We must fulfill the second half of Romans 8:1 to experience the freedom of the first part.

Many quote, **"There is no condemnation for those who are in Christ Jesus."** This is true if we walk according to the Spirit and not according to the flesh. How many though are walking according to the flesh, living under condemnation and wonder what is wrong with their faith? It's not their faith, it's rather their flesh and sin that is controlling them instead of the Spirit of God. Our flesh must die so that His Spirit comes alive in us and we live in victory and not condemnation. The reason the condemnation remains is because guilt remains because the flesh keeps giving in. We must be set free by Christ and walk by the power of the Holy Spirit.

Back to Psalm 37:4. You see, to see the desires of our heart come to pass, we must first delight ourselves in the One who made us, formed us and knows us better than anybody. He already knows our desires, all He asks is that our hearts delight in Him…and Him alone. When we do, His desires will then become our desires.

It reminds me of what Christ said in Matthew 6:33.

> ***Seek first the Kingdom of God and His righteousness and all these things shall be added unto you.***

Jesus already knows about "***all these things***" in our hearts. But what He desires first is for us to seek His kingdom and righteousness in our lives. If we do, then "***all these things***" begin to flow into our lives because they start to align themselves with God's best for us.

I believe our Heavenly Father wants to bless His children with good things. Remember what Jesus said in Matthew 7:9?

> ***Or what man is there among you who, if his son asks for bread, will give him a stone? Or if he asks for a fish, will he give him a serpent? If you then, being evil, know how to give good gifts to your children, how much more will your Father who is in heaven give good things to those who ask Him!***

The team riding today also had a chance to once again meet up with the Father/Son team of *"Mike and Big Mike."* It was heart warming to watch a dad support his son and ride behind him in the support vehicle at a very slow speed with his flashers on while his boy pedaled in front of him. Mike's reason for riding was to raise awareness and money for kids with epilepsy.

Our Mission 66 team also passed out many tracts and had the opportunity to talk with people along the journey today. One gentleman that I spoke with today was named Frank. As he walked by the roadside, I decided to stop and introduce myself and share our reason for the ride. I also learned about Frank's story. My conversation with him made my heart heavy.

You see, when I began to speak to Frank about Jesus and the need we have for forgiveness, Frank said he couldn't do it because of all the "*bad things*" that he has done in his life. He said he would feel like such a hypocrite. I tried to explain how Christ took all our sin, no matter how "*bad or wrong*", and nailed it to the cross so that we could be forgiven of anything.

> ***If we confess our sins, He is faithful and just to forgive us our sins and to cleanse us from all unrighteousness. -1 John 1:9***

Frank just couldn't do it. He shook my hand, thanked me for stopping and we went our separate ways. Oh Lord, touch Frank and remind him of Your love and that he's not too far away or too bad that he can't be forgiven. Only You can convince him.

Another man I met today had a name that you would only find in this neck of the woods. His name was *"Dusty Phillips."* His name made me smile because I don't think I would ever meet someone with a cool name like that in Central Pennsylvania.

All in all, it was a good day. We rode past the Oklahoma border into Shamrock, Texas, but spent the night at an RV site just back over the border in Texola, Oklahoma. Tonight, we would have dinner at the Windmill Restaurant.

The Lord has been so faithful today in so many ways. Not only today, but this entire trip. Not only this entire trip, but my entire life. Sometimes I just have to stop and thank Him for how He watched over me even before I knew Him or was following Him with my life. It reminds me of the verse found in 2 Timothy 2:13 that says,

> ***If we are faithless, He remains faithful; He cannot deny Himself.***

So glad that even when we're faithless, God always remains faithful.

CHAPTER 6
TEXAS...HALF WAY THERE!!

Day 16 - Thursday, September 21st

Today was one hot, windy day in the Lone Star State! I remember these Texas roads from three years ago when Harold and I biked across America. The people were great, the roads not so much. In 2014, we biked through the hill country and spent one third of our days (13 of 38) in Texas on our way from Santa Monica to Saint Augustine. This time we would skirt along the panhandle for only a couple of days, which was more than enough for me.

The day began as we put our gear on and began pedaling before the sun even peaked over the horizon. We were greeted by a dazzling array of stars in the beautiful Texas morning sky. Things do look bigger in Texas!

As the sun began to rise, the beauty of the colors burst on the scene. What a way to start a day, even if it was about 3:30 or 4 in the morning! I find the more I can slow down and enjoy these moments, the more contentment and peace I seem to experience in my life. The Lord has created so many good things for our enjoyment, and I believe we miss so many of them because of our fast paced life. It seems to me that the more advanced we become with technology to help us save time and be more efficient, the less time we actually have to relax and connect with the One who created everything before us that we see.

Today would be one of those days where we didn't see many people for long stretches of riding on open roads with not much around us. On top of this, the winds picked up as we pedaled into the afternoon, something that was becoming common on this trip. This also made the enjoyment of the day, well, not that enjoyable.

The combination of these things as well as the heat began to take its toll on me today. But as we rode, I was encouraged by Joel as he quoted Isaiah 40:31 and Dalton as he reminded me of the Cross and Crucifixion scene that we had just seen in Groom, Texas. Sensing my weakness, Joel and Dalton began to encourage my mind and heart as they shared these things with me. What a blessing to have a team of people to help lift you up when you're feeling down or weak. Don't we all need that in our lives?

Earlier in the day we met two pastors, Andy and Micah, who invited us into their air-conditioned church building to get refreshed and enjoy our lunch. We were sitting outside the church changing yet another flat. We're continually amazed how the Lord keeps placing the right people in our paths at just the right time. But then again, why should that surprise us?

Remember when Peter and John prayed for the lame man by the Temple Gate called Beautiful? *(Acts 3)* He was healed, and the people were amazed! Peter asked them, *"Why do you marvel at this?" (Acts 3:12)*. In Peter's words I hear him saying that we should expect God

Texas...Half Way There!!

to work in these ways on our behalf, not surprised when He does so. This should be *"normal Christianity."* We need not be surprised when the Lord does such things, but rather rejoice in knowing this is God's plan for us all along.

The Cross we saw today in Groom, Texas stood 190 feet tall. You can see it from really faraway. My prayer is that as we continue the second half of this journey, that more people would come to recognize and see the work that Christ did for them on the Cross at Calvary.

Have you? If you haven't, why not take a moment and ask Him to become a part of your journey and invite Him to be your Lord and Savior? If you do, I guarantee you that you'll marvel at the gift of forgiveness and the price He paid for you on the cross. And as you begin to follow Him with your days, you will see Him work miracles in your life in ways that will make you stand amazed. But don't be surprised, that's what He has been desiring to do in your life all along.

Once again, I reflect on the Lord's healing of my shoulder today and was grateful to be able to ride again. His blessings in our lives are evident every day, if we can slow down enough to recognize them.

Day 17 - Friday, September 22nd

Midpoint! Today would be the day that we reach the exact midpoint on our journey, 1,139 miles from where we began in Chicago and where we'll end in Los Angeles.

Our Only Hope

The town, Adrian Texas. The café at this midpoint is bustling! But what caught my attention more than anything, was the sign in this restaurant's window.

Once again, this confirmed the reason that fifteen people chose to travel along with me on this journey. The reason for our trip was staring at us as we walked through the door of this café. We also had the privilege of meeting more wonderful people from around the world. Dillan and Erik, from Germany, were on this route and another young man, Kristian, would become a friend of ours for the remainder of the trip. Kristian was from Denmark and decided to go on an adventure.

Hey, why not, right? Life's too short to not have some adventures, right? He decided to fly to New York City, lay down some cash on a bike and pedal his way across America to the Pacific Coast. Lloyd had invited him to join us for lunch. Kristian would then ride with us the rest of the day and over the next few days we would re-connect with him here and there. Eventually, he became a part of our team and would pedal with us the rest of the trip.

Our landing spot for the night would place us in our sixth state, New Mexico, as we ended the day in Tucumcari. Once again, the winds were strong, about 20MPH, which made us work for every mile we pedaled. Pastor Derek warmly welcomed us to stay at his place for the night as we set up camp in his drive and his church also

Texas...Half Way There!!

blessed our team with a couple of hotel rooms. I've been overwhelmed at people's hospitality this entire trip.

Pastor Derek also took care of us with an Italian dinner for the entire team, my favorite! The sunset this evening was incredible. Morning would arrive much too soon, but we would enjoy a slower start to the day. Pastor Derek made arrangements for breakfast with he and a friend, Brandon, who owned a bike shop in town. What a great place to land for the night. Once again, our hearts, and stomachs, were full.

Our Only Hope

CHAPTER 7
NEW MEXICO...FINDING REST

Day 18 - Saturday, September 23rd

There's just something about a Saturday morning and a good, hearty breakfast. Pastor Derek and Brandon would treat our entire team to a wonderful start to our day at the "*Kix on 66*" restaurant. The town of Tucumcari we understand is rather desolate compared to a few years back, but one stop that you must make if you ever travel through this part of the country is the *"Blue Swallow Hotel."*

Our Only Hope

The forecast called for clouds and rain, and it did not disappoint. This made the decision to not be in such a hurry much easier. Following breakfast we swung by Brandon's place, the *"B-Diggity Bike Shop."* He looked over some of our bikes and then he and Derek helped shuttle us to our starting point for the day.

The ride today was miserable, although some seemed to enjoy the rain. I admit, I'm a *"fair weather rider."* So when thunder and lightning struck near where I was riding, I quickly hopped in the support van for a few miles. Sometimes you hear the Lord's voice, and sometimes you hear your wife's voice from thousands of miles away say, *"Get in the van!"* Today would also greet me with two flat tires, and to top off the day, when we arrived at the RV park for the night, a dog found a liking to my ankles and knees.

The most memorable part of my day was when we chose a more direct route to ride. These desolate roads were very wet and sandy which made it difficult to just roll along on the bikes. We noticed in the distance a few ranchers driving cattle up over the hill. This was a picture I'll not quickly forget, so I paused to just *"be still and know that He was God."*

I really needed this peaceful moment as I motioned to the guys with me to just keep riding. Quiet, still, peaceful. I stood and watched and listened to the silence and simply took in God's presence for a few moments. I picked up a rock to take home with me that now sits on a shelf in my office. On it I wrote...

Be still and know that I am God. -Psalm 46:10

The day would end as we met some wonderful people from Santa Rosa First Assembly of God as they invited us to dinner at a Mexican restaurant. Another day in the books!

Day 19 - Sunday, September 24th

I decided to go for an early walk into town and then find my way to the church. The town was small, there were many abandoned buildings and it was a Sunday morning with very few cars on the road. I found myself walking further than expected until I found a place called the *"Blue Hole."*

This spot is, well - a blue hole. 81 feet deep, 60 feet in diameter and 61 degrees all the time. People were scuba diving when I arrived. I climbed above the hole and simply sat on the edge of one of the rocks and read Psalm 46, overlooking the scene below me.

As I sat here, the Lord began to stir a different message in my heart that I would preach this morning. It would simply be titled, *"Be Still."*

I began my walk back towards town in the direction of the church. Along the way I stopped to enjoy a hot breakfast at a

Our Only Hope

restaurant where I was able to meet a waitress named Megan and share with her a few thoughts about the Lord and His love for her.

Kristian would also meet up with us again and join us in worship at the First Assembly of God. He didn't grow up in a Christian home, so it was great to have him worship with us this morning. We had a good service with the people and then a family in the church invited our team over to their ranch for lunch. My wife must have called ahead because…spaghetti was on the menu!

It was once again a blessing to watch as the Lord provided for our team. One of her sons was even a professional biker and *"just so happened"* to have a bike stand to work on bikes and the tools that were needed to make some repairs. In a heartbeat, our *"bike mechanic,"* Lloyd, went to work on Zjelko's bike.

These Sabbath days renew our strength, and we would need it as we had a very hard week ahead of us. I've come to realize on both of these long, mission trips how much it means to rest your body. The Scriptures teach us much about our bodies and the need for rest.

I realize the culture that we live in prevents everyone from resting on Sundays. However, may I ask when is your Sabbath? What one day of your week looks much different than the other six and allows you time to slow down, relax and rejuvenate?

A friend of mine in ministry, Rich Earl, has many thoughts about the importance of rest and caring for our bodies. Over the past decade or so, Rich has begun taking care of his body in earnest and enjoying the great outdoors as he straps on his boots and hikes through the woods. I believe that Rich has learned the secret of getting alone with the Lord, being still and knowing that He is God. He has learned the benefits of rest, of slowing down long enough to hear from the Lord. Sometimes we slow down, but not quite long enough to hear His voice. I encourage you to take time to find your way and establish restful patterns in your days. It does the body, soul and mind very good. Here are some verses that speak to us about the importance of rest.

> ***Come to Me, all you who labor and are heavy laden, and I will give you rest.* -Matthew 11:28**

New Mexico...Finding Rest

> *Take My yoke upon you and learn from Me, for I am gentle and lowly in heart, and you will find rest for your souls. -Matthew 11:29*

> *Rest in the Lord and wait patiently for Him. -Psalm 37:7*

And this verse says it all!

> *And on the seventh day God ended His work which He had done, and He rested on the seventh day from all His work which He had done. -Genesis 2:2*

Hey, if God needed a break, don't we? Seriously though, we know He didn't need to rest. He didn't stop after the first six days and say, *"Man, that creation thing was hard, I need a break."* It was His way of setting an example for us.

Rest does so much good for our bodies and without it we become less productive, we grow weaker in our souls and more prone to temptation and – GRUMPY! Running ourselves weary leaves us open to the enemy's attacks. Restoring our bodies and souls weekly gives us health and strength to overcome. Let's make a habit of carving some time into our weekly schedules to kick back and take it easy.

Ok, back on the bike.

As we continue our journey through our fifth state, New Mexico, I'm watching as the Lord fulfills this verse before us each and every day.

> *A man's heart plans his way, But the Lord directs his steps. -Proverbs 16:9*

We chose a place for dinner and quickly found out that the Lord directed us to exactly where He wanted us. You see, I believe that even the places we eat at are directed by the Lord because we have a waitress or waiter that will be serving us that we have the privilege of blessing and getting to know.

On a side note, when eating out, let's remember to treat our servers well. My kids have both worked in this industry for many years and have unfortunately had some very unpleasant experiences

Our Only Hope

with people that have grown very impatient when it comes to food. They've also shared stories of the kindness and generosity of those who bless them in ways they weren't expecting. Your kindness, generosity and patience (even if they don't refill your cup as soon as you think it should be filled) will speak volumes! Oh, and leave a nice tip, especially if you are trying to be a light for Jesus while you are there.

At the restaurant tonight, our waiter's name was John. We asked if there was anything we could pray for as we paused to give thanks for our meal. He was moved by this because he said that he had been *"praying for someone to come into his life that would pray for his mom."* She was having tests tomorrow due to a recent heart attack. John stayed near as we prayed for our meal, and for his mom, Tammy. John seemed overwhelmed at how the Lord brought this group of people into the restaurant tonight. I believe the Lord simply directed our steps. John was so excited that he called his mom on the phone and had me talk with her. It also gave me a chance to pray with her directly over the phone.

I truly thank the Lord for the good day of worship, rest and ministry. I join with the Psalmist as he begins and ends Psalm 118 by declaring:

> **Oh, give thanks to the Lord, for He is good! For His mercy endures forever.**

Day 20 - Monday, September 25th

Today we traverse the edge of the Rocky Mountains. There were some tough climbs, but you know what they say, *"What goes up, must come down."* And the down part? Wow! The only problem is they don't last nearly as long as the upward climb that comes right before them. In life, that's true as well at times.

It seems like adversities and trials take such hard work to climb over, but if we can hold on and keep climbing, He is a rewarder of good things and will provide relief on the other side of the mountain. But while we're climbing, let's not forget that the victory has already been provided by Christ at Calvary. Let's fight through in His strength, not ours. We'll wear out and quit if we try to climb these hills on our own. But as we stop trying so hard in our own strength and rely on His, we will find His strength to overcome. I mentioned previously that a friend of mine once said, *"We fight from victory, not for victory."*

Climbing builds strength, character and teaches us how to rely on Christ to overcome adversity. Truth be told, when I ride, I only grow stronger when I climb hills. The down hills are incredibly fun, but they don't make me one bit stronger.

Paul writes about this in Romans 5:3-5.

> **And not only that, but we also glory in tribulations, knowing that tribulation produces perseverance; and perseverance, character; and character, hope. Now hope does not disappoint, because the love of God has been poured out in our hearts by the Holy Spirit who was given to us.**

Don't ever lose hope, because hope keeps you going and does not disappoint. Why? Because the love of God has been poured into our hearts by the Holy Spirit.

I often think of Job when I think of the ups and downs of life. He surely had reason to lose hope and give up. He had three *"friends"* who thought he must've done something wrong and a wife who told him to curse God and die. Nice, huh? Through ups and downs in life, Job held onto the Lord God Almighty.

Did he have questions? Sure, he actually asked *"why"* seven times in chapter 3 of Job. But Job never allowed his *"whys"* to turn into accusations against God. Did he have answers? Not right away. Did

God speak and come through? Yes, in His timing. And His timing will be perfect in your life as well.

You see, character building is never easy. Glance back and take a moment to read those verses from Romans 5 again. Tribulations and trials are no fun, but necessary to grow. The Lord is always there with us, walking through these things we face in life. He is developing us, shaping us, pruning us. Does it hurt at times? Absolutely! But just wait and see what He does on the other side when you're flying down that hill. Hold on, it will be a good ride!

Day 21 - Tuesday, September 26th

Forty-four degrees, damp and breezy is not my idea of a fun morning for biking. Some love it. For me, give me eighty degrees and sunny. But one thing did warm us up as we began our day. A man who was camping near us, Bob, came over to our group as we were getting ready and prayed for us before we left. Encouragement from others along the way is sometimes the very thing we need to keep going.

Another believer who blessed us today was a business owner, Carlos, at a convenience store along the way. He said to pick out whatever breakfast sandwiches we wanted. As I asked him about the Lord, he responded confidently and with great excitement, "*I already have Jesus in my heart.*"

We ended our day in Albuquerque, New Mexico at the home of Mitchell and Ashley and their two boys. We were connected with them through Pastor Derek back in Tucumcari. Todd Pugh, who would be joining us in a few days was also instrumental in making some of these connections for us through this part of the country. He and Pastor Derek are brother-in-laws. What a great meal they ordered out for us as we enjoyed some pizza and subs. What a blessing to be encouraged and helped by so many along the way.

We find in Scripture how the Apostle Paul was encouraged by so many along his journey.

> **For I long to see you, that I may impart to you some spiritual gift, so that you may be established – that is, that I**

may be encouraged together with you by the mutual faith both of you and me. -Romans 1:11, 12

What a statement! Do you think Paul needed encouraged? He was stoned, beaten, whipped, shipwrecked, along with many other adversities that came his way. But he was encouraged by those of mutual faith. And so are we.

Too many people stop fellowship and worship all together when life gets hard. That's the very time that we need to push in more and be around those of *"mutual faith"* to encourage us in our time of need.

And let us consider one another in order to stir up love and good works, not forsaking the assembling of ourselves together, as is the manner of some, but exhorting one another, and so much the more as you see the Day approaching. -Hebrews 10:24, 25

As believers and followers of Christ, we must make a point to encourage one another. Let's not give up assembling together as we see the Day of the Lord and His return getting closer. Don't allow the enemy to isolate you, it's a trick he uses to ruin many in their walks with Christ. Think of the nature shows that we've watched where the lion finds an isolated animal that is alone outside the herd…it usually doesn't end well! We must pursue Christ and gather together with other believers (our herd) to encourage us, protect us and provide fellowship in our walk with Him…and do so even more as we see the Day approaching.

Will there be times that we're hurt, disappointed and overlooked? Sure, but let us keep our eyes on Jesus and not place any person on a pedestal. Don't allow our expectations of others to get so high that we're disappointed, hurt and tempted to quit.

Day 22 - Wednesday, September 27th

My good friend, Gary, would head back to Pennsylvania today. I came to realize once again how hard it is to say good-bye as I drove him to the airport early this morning.

Our Only Hope

But for all things, there is a season. Solomon, whom the Bibles refers to as the wisest person to ever live, talks about the "*seasons*" we go through in life.

> *To everything there is a season, a time for every purpose under heaven:*
>
> *A time to be born, and a time to die;*
>
> *A time to plant, and a time to pluck what is planted;*
>
> *A time to kill, and a time to heal;*
>
> *A time to break down, and a time to build up;*
>
> *A time to weep, and a time to laugh;*
>
> *A time to mourn, and a time to dance;*
>
> *A time to cast away stones, and a time to gather stones;*
>
> *A time to embrace, and a time to refrain from embracing;*
>
> *A time to gain, and a time to lose;*
>
> *A time to keep, and a time to throw away;*
>
> *A time to tear, and a time to sew;*
>
> *A time to keep silence, and a time to speak;*
>
> *A time to love, and a time to hate;*
>
> *A time of war, and a time of peace.*
>
> *-Ecclesiastes 3:1-8*

I write more about these verses in a previous book called, *"Minutes Matter...Making Every Beat Count."* Seasons come and go so quickly in all of our lives. Looking back over the years, my wife and I have walked through the seasons of being newlyweds, having kids, watching them grow, marry, and now the so called *"empty nest."* Don't get me wrong, we love our kids, but the season of the empty nest is not so bad! Hey, it's a good thing we still like each other!

I believe a key to enjoying every season we're in has to do with a few things.

One, remember the past just long enough, but don't *"camp out"* there.

Two, focus on doing what the Lord wants you to do in the season you currently find yourself in.

Three, continue to dream about your future. You see, if you get stuck in the past you can never enjoy the present or the future. If you're always dreaming about your future, you can also rob yourself of enjoying the present. And if you drive yourself day in and day out to only get through today, you will lose passion for life and not enjoy the moments of yesterday and tomorrow. In other words, strive to keep your perspective on life and the seasons you pass through in balance.

On the way back from dropping Gary off at the airport, I had a chance to stop by and speak with a man who was on the median of the road. His name was Robert, and during this season in his life, he found himself homeless. He was a Christian man with two daughters.

As I spoke to him, he was very encouraging because of his love for the Lord and his daughters, even in the midst of this hard season he found himself in. I was able to give him a few bucks to help him out and also asked if he had a Bible. He said he did and that he also reads his Daily Bread every day. It's funny, when you stop to help someone, many times they bless you just by hearing their story. Robert found himself at peace and content with this season of life.

Our Only Hope

But how? He was homeless and had very little. I believe he could only do so as he put into practice what the Apostle Paul spoke of in **Philippians 4:11-13**.

> **Not that I speak in regard to need, for I have learned in whatever state I am, to be content. I know how to be abased, and I know how to abound. Everywhere and in all things I have learned both to be full and to be hungry, both to abound and to suffer need. I can do all things through Christ who strengthens me.**

Most of us are aware of verse thirteen, but as we look closely at verses eleven and twelve, we begin to fully understand what Paul is saying. Paul could do all things and find contentment in Christ, whether he had little or much…was full or hungry. In other words, no matter what the circumstance or season of life Paul found himself in, he found contentment through the only One who could provide it.

What season are you in? Are you at peace in your heart? Do you find yourself content? If not, the only way to find it is through Christ. In the words of Princess Buttercup's Westley. *"Life is pain, Highness. Anyone who says differently is selling something."* [1] Many times life is good, but other times it's not. But we can do all things through Christ who strengthens us, in all circumstances and situations we find ourselves in.

As I returned from dropping Gary off at the airport, Ralph and Sherie would shuttle me to the where the bikers were at this point. The day was cold and rainy again! I must say I was not disappointed that I missed some of the earlier miles. But what was about to happen next would make the day all worth-while.

We stopped at a convenience store/gas station in the town of Cubero, New Mexico. The name of the store was *"Village de Cubero."* One of the workers at the store educated us on some of the history of this place by sharing how Ernest Hemingway had completed some of his writings here and how *"Ricky and Lucy"* had spent the night at their bed and breakfast many years ago. Pretty high stuff for a place in the middle of nowhere.

New Mexico...Finding Rest

But what was about to transpire would top any of the things that ever took place here. A man pulled in to fill up his tank. I went over to talk to this man and Brian joined me in the conversation as well. He was a Native American and went by the name of *"LeWayne."* He spoke of how he was forced to grow up in a specific denomination and he ultimately rejected religion altogether. He began to open up about his upbringing.

At first he seemed very hard and against even talking about *"religion."* In so many words we shared with him how a *"relationship with Christ"* was different from *"religion."* Brian and I had a front row seat as we watched his heart begin to soften. We spoke to him about how we had prayed before this trip that the Lord would bring the right people across our path.

LeWayne realized that being there with us at the exact same time was impossible without the Lord's hand in it. We said, *"the Lord brought us on this trip for people just like you."* The next thing we know, this man's heart began to change and he said, *"I'm just tired,"* and that *"he didn't want to live like this any longer."* He began to weep as we watched the Holy Spirit soften his heart. Only Jesus can do that. What a moment! The Lord then impressed upon my heart to share these words of Jesus with him:

> **Come unto Me, all you who labor and are heavy laden, and I will give you rest. -Matthew 11:28**

We asked him about trusting in Christ with his life and invited him to pray with us to begin that journey with Jesus. What a moment as he prayed with us to ask for Christ's forgiveness and invite Him into his life! And to think, I could've missed it. I mean, the weather did turn miserable and I really didn't feel like riding. On top of that, I was really missing my wife today. I thanked the Lord for reminding me once again that this was not about my bike, but about the people. My prayer is that this man will grow in his faith by reading the Gospel of John we gave him and find a good place to worship...and continue to find his rest in Christ.

Our Only Hope

This day reminded me of a story that Lloyd shared with me of a friend who had a dream about going to heaven. His friend told him that it changed how he viewed sharing his faith. In his dream, when he got there, he realized that his house was the only one there from his neighborhood that he lived in while on earth. He then asked the Lord, "W*hy aren't any of the other houses from my neighborhood here?"* And Jesus said, "B*ecause you didn't share Me with any of them."*

May we take time and share Jesus with those around us every day. Whether riding a bike on Route 66, talking with our co-workers or neighbors, or simply sharing Christ's love with whomever He puts in your path that day. Let's make a point to take time to share Jesus so that when we get to heaven we will see the influence we had in people making a decision to be there as well.

Sometimes I wonder why it says in **Revelation 21:4** that He will *"wipe away every tear from our eyes."* Could it be because of the people we should have shared Jesus with, but didn't? Let's take time, no matter the cost, and share with others who are lost and hurting.

Day 23 - Thursday, September 28th

The day started out cold and wet from all the rain the previous day. Starting to notice a pattern? We decided to start a little later, but not as early as Lloyd who again rolled out around 5:30am. The rest of the team would begin around 9am, but even at this time, the temperatures were in the mid-40's and the cold, wet weather made it feel much worse. Before we began this trip, I never anticipated the temperatures being this cold. I then thought *"How did Lloyd do this four hours earlier?"*

We would also find ourselves at the highest point of our journey today. The *"Continental Divide"* at this point of the country sits at 7,882 feet above sea level.

Today would challenge us with some tough climbs, but also some fantastic downhill rides! We saw very few people on these desolate roads, but the few that we did encounter gave us a chance to pass out more of the "*Mission 66*" tracts.

One man we met, George, mentioned to us how at one point in his life he was an alcoholic but had not touched a drink in thirty years. Lloyd had already accomplished a few "*hundred mile days*," but today would be the first century ride of the trip for Joel, Dalton and myself. We really wanted a hundred miler today, so much that we got two flat tires during the last five miles and still took time to change them. I know it's only a number, but for some reason it feels so good to accomplish one hundred miles in one day.

Every day has been a testimony of God's protection over our team. Today was especially true as He protected us during this cold day on the wet and rainy roads. Dalton was also protected from getting clipped by a car. It was a day that we found God's faithfulness once again over our team and reminded me of the verse found in Psalm 46:1.

> **God is our refuge and strength, A very present help in trouble.**

Day 24 - Friday, September 29th

Last night we stayed at the "*USA RV Park*" before we pedaled west toward Holbrook, New Mexico this morning. Within minutes of being on the bikes, there were a few people along the roads that we had a chance to meet. In Austin's video last night, I shared about how some that may be watching this may be feeling tired and weary. As we pedaled down the road, one of the first guys I spoke to echoed this thought. He wearily voiced, *"I'm just tired."* It was a common thread I was beginning to hear from several people. Early on in my walk with Christ, one of my favorite verses became what Jesus said in Matthew 11:28.

> **Come to Me, all you who labor and are heavy laden, and I will give you rest.**

Our Only Hope

How often do we ignore this invitation from Jesus to *"come and find rest?"* How often do we keep going at a breakneck pace only to sometimes crash and burn? How often do we labor and carry things around that weigh us down when all the while Jesus is saying, *"Come to Me….I'll give you rest."* Not only rest, but also look at the next two verses.

> ***Take My yoke upon you and learn from Me, for I am gentle and lowly in heart, and you will find rest for your souls. For My yoke is easy and My burden is light.***
> ***-Matthew 11:29, 30***

I remember training for the first bike trip across country, *"Coast 2 Coast 4 Jesus."* I was invited to take part in a *"bootcamp"* at 5:30 in the morning! Joan was our trainer, and she would push us to the max and challenge us to the core. One time, we were carrying sand bags up and down a set of stairs. Seriously…at 5:30 in the morning! Those things were heavy and no fun at all. It felt so good when she said to *"drop them."* The weight I was carrying was no longer. I didn't argue with her and ask to carry them a little further. Nope, when she said *"done,"* I was *"done."*

So why is it when Jesus invites us to come to him, drop the weights at His feet and allow Him to carry them for us, that we choose to keep them on our shoulders?

We all have the choice and privilege to know Jesus. To allow Him to carry our burdens. To learn from Him and not continue in our own stubborn ways. He reminds us that His yoke is easy and His burden is light. I don't know about you, but any burden that I carry is never light. But when we give that burden to Jesus, He takes it from us and then we can find that Jesus, not the burden you were once carrying, brings a lightness to your soul. You find rest in knowing that all is well. But it's only when *you* come to Jesus…and no one will force you, you must choose to do so.

Some of you reading this right now need to drop the weights. Your burdens are overwhelming. You need to come to Jesus. You're tired just like these ones I've met over the past couple of days. Here are two guarantees to choose from.

1) Don't come to Jesus and you will never find rest for your soul.
2) Come to Jesus and you will always find rest for your soul.

Why not take a moment if you're feeling burdened and come to Jesus. Set this book down, pick up your Bible and spend some time allowing Jesus to refresh and renew your strength. I love what we read in one of the most popular chapters in the Bible. Most of the times we hear it read at funerals, but really, it's good for everyday life.

> *He makes me to lie down in green pastures; He leads me beside the still waters. He restores my soul...*
> *-Psalm 23:2, 3(a)*

I remember a time years ago when I used to go regularly with a chair, my Bible, a good book, some water and snacks and sit by a stream. (You have to have snacks!) I would read, I would pray and be refreshed. Life gets busy, life gets crazy, life gets heavy. Jesus is the only One that can carry our burdens and restore our soul. Is it time for you to have your soul restored? Allow the Holy Spirit and the Word to renew your soul right now.

Following the start to the day, a few of the guys missed a turn in the road and kept riding when they were supposed to turn left. Joel also got a flat tire at the same time. These delays caused us to fall behind, but they were all part of God's bigger plan.

As most of the team pedaled ahead, Joel and I lagged behind as we talked about life side by side. That's when we came upon a turn in the road and a guy walking towards us pointed in the direction that the guys ahead of us had gone. We decided to stop and meet this man, whose name was Vincent. And the thought hit me, *"We would've never ran across him had the guys not gone down a wrong road and Joel didn't have another flat tire."*

As we began conversation with Vincent, we shared with him the reason for our ride and asked him about knowing Jesus Christ in his life. He said that his wife, who was a believer, had been talking to

Our Only Hope

him about knowing Christ in his life. At that moment, I believe he realized how we were placed on that road for this exact reason. For him to come to Jesus. We offered Vincent the opportunity to accept Christ and find forgiveness and he decided to take us up on the offer. What a moment! I just wish I could've been in his home when he told his wife what happened today. Oh, how the Lord has a way of getting our attention when we least expect it.

Shortly up the road, we met a couple named Edmund and Renee, who were getting married on Monday. What a blessing to pray for their upcoming marriage before we pedaled on. It truly was a great day of ministry on the roads.

One other highlight happened as we were blessed to pedal through the *"National Petrified Forest."* Petrified was a good word today during the ride through this park as thunder and lightning was all around us and it sent me into the van for part of the ride. Some of the others braved it out. I was just hearing my wife's voice once again from thousands of miles away saying, *"Get. In. The. Van. Now."* I had no problem obeying the voice. And now I hear her saying, *"I wish you would listen to me just as easily at home."* Yes, dear.

New Mexico...Finding Rest

CHAPTER 8
ARIZONA...ALMOST THERE!

Day 25 - Saturday, September 30th

Another flat tire…another divine appointment. They slow us down, but always seem to be for a reason. As we slept last night, it seems that one of our biker's tires decided to allow all the air to leak out. By this point, we've lost track of how many flat tires Joel has experienced.

It's no fun to wake up to a flat tire even before your day gets going. Some of the other bikers hit the road as Joel and I fixed the tire. We then got started and as we biked into town, we came across a man walking around the corner directly towards us. We stopped to talk with him and quickly found out the reason for the delay this morning. Once again, we realized how God's ways are higher and much greater than our limited knowledge.

> *For as the heavens are higher than the earth, So are My ways higher than your ways, And My thoughts than your thoughts. -Isaiah 55:9*

Dean shared with us how he is a believer in the Lord, but could be doing much better in his walk with Him. So true of all of us, right? But what we all need from time to time is someone to come alongside of us and say, *"It's okay, come on, get back on track, the Lord forgives you and wants to see you healthy again."* It reminds me of when Peter was in need of restoration after denying that he even knew Christ. Remember that scene after the resurrection? The last time Peter had seen Christ was immediately following denying Him three times and Jesus locked eyes with him. Imagine this scene.

> *And the Lord turned and looked at Peter. Then Peter remembered the word of the Lord, how He had said to him, "Before the rooster crows, you will deny Me three times." So Peter went out and wept bitterly. -Luke 22:61, 62*

Peter was distraught and guilt ridden. He truly needed an encouraging word that the Lord still loved him and wanted to use him. After the resurrection, John records for us the wonderful restoration of Peter. (John 21:15-17) Three times Jesus asks Peter the question, *"do you love Me?"* Here are Peter's three responses:

> *"Yes, Lord; You know that I love You."*

> *"Yes, Lord; You know that I love You."*

> *"Lord, You know all things; You know that I love You."*

Three times Peter denied the Lord, but three times the Lord asks the question and restores Peter. Each time after Peter's response, the Lord *then* asks Peter to do something.

> *"Feed My lambs."*

> *"Tend My sheep."*

> *"Feed My sheep."*

Arizona...Almost There!

Saying something is one thing, but following through and doing something about it is quite another. Now we know that we aren't saved by what we do, but what we do is proof of the living relationship that we have with our Savior. Jesus restored Peter, and now asked him to do something.

As we spent a few moments on that corner and then pedaled away, I was reminded of what I heard in a sermon once. The preacher said, *"You must continue to read God's Word because it's God's Word that continues to read us."*

I believe this is where the strength of our relationship begins and ends. When we have regular time in the presence of Jesus and His Word, we grow and become stronger. And when we aren't following through with this pattern in our lives, we tend to become weaker and less content.

We took time to pray for Dean and when we finished, he hugged us, wiped a tear from his eye...and we pedaled on our way. Once again, a flat tire equaled another divine appointment.

> **Now thanks be to God who always leads us in triumph in Christ, and through us diffuses the fragrance of His knowledge in every place. -2 Corinthians 2:14**

We must realize that where we go, He is wanting to lead us, give us victory and allow His fragrance to be diffused all around us. We would need this once again at the end of the day.

We arrived in Flagstaff at Mountain View Assembly of God, where we planned to set up camp and spend the night. However, the place we were supposed to park was not long enough and too narrow. We searched online for other options to camp and another explored the option of a different church's parking lot. We then prayed, *"Lord, show us and lead us to the right place."*

All the RV parks were pretty full due to a home NAU football game in town. But the Lord led us to a very nice campground for a modest $32.50/night...for everyone! The name was *"Black Bart's RV Park."* God is so good! Once again, we saw God's hand at work as He provided a great place for us to spend the next two nights. As we got settled, we then took the afternoon to head to the Grand Canyon and see God's amazing handiwork. What a treat!

In the beginning, God created the heavens and the earth.
-Genesis 1:1

Day 26 - Sunday, October 1st

It was a beautiful morning, so I decided to walk to church, which was about two miles away. On the way, I came across a man, Jorge, who was homeless and also a believer. As he glanced at the Mission 66 tract and saw the name Jesus, he said to me, *"Christo numero uno."* I didn't need to know *"mucho Espanol"* to know what he was saying.

One thing I've come to realize on this trip is that those who have very little usually possess very much in their love for Jesus. I find the same to be true when I make my twice yearly trips to Africa with Haven of Hope Global Ministries.

Jesus said in Luke 12:15,

...one's life does not consist in the abundance of the things he possesses.

As I handed him a $5 bill, you'd have thought that I'd given him the world. For me, it was much more gratifying than the five I would lay down at the Starbucks just a few minutes later.

I arrived early at the *"Mountaintop Assembly of God"* church where I was preaching that morning.

Arizona...Almost There!

This morning I would preach the message, "*Great is Your Faithfulness.*"

The Lord used the message and a handful of people responded to salvation. What a blessing it was to also see people around the altars who made their way forward to be refreshed by the Holy Spirit. We were very grateful for Pastor Jackie and his congregation.

It was also a special treat for us to meet one of fourteen remaining *"Navajo Code Talkers"* in the world, who was in the worship service this morning. Samuel Sandoval was one of four hundred who voluntarily helped America in World War II. Thank you, Samuel, for serving our country in the way that you did. It was a very special moment for Brian as he always wanted to meet one of these brave men. And there he was. Once again, the Lord had us at just the right place at just the right time.

Following service we had lunch at another "*Triple D*" restaurant called, "*Salsa Brava.*" The Grande Burrito was amazing. But something memorable happened here that was a first on this trip... Dalton ordered a meal that he could not finish! This boy can eat! Let's just say I'm glad I don't have his grocery bill every month.

Following lunch, some of the team would ride into Sedona to take in the beautiful red rocks and breathtaking scenery. I would head to the airport to pick up a friend, Todd Pugh, who would join us for the remainder of the trip. It was a blessing to have him join the

Our Only Hope

team and we would actually end this journey on his birthday at the Pacific Ocean.

One week to go! It's been almost a month since we left Pennsylvania and our loved ones. My wife is such a source of strength for me here on earth. She believes in me, she trusts me, she respects and encourages me to follow the dreams the Lord places on my heart. I could go on and on. But the one thing I appreciate about her maybe more than anything is her faithfulness. Both to the Lord over all these years and to our relationship and marriage. I know that she prays for me, supports me, loves me and would do anything for me.

> **He who finds a wife finds a good thing, And obtains favor from the Lord. -Proverbs 18:22**

I'm very grateful that the Lord chose her for me. She has followed the Lord's calling on our lives, when I'm sure it felt to her that it was a calling on "*my life*." She has never objected to the Lord's will when she truly knew it was Him leading us in a certain direction. Only about a week to go till I see her waiting at the Pittsburgh airport!

Lord, give our team strength for this last week. Continue to watch over us, I thank you for your care and protection over the team to this point. May You continue to guide us to the people You would want us to meet this last week of the journey.

Day 27 - Monday, October 2nd

The first day of our last week began this morning. Todd and I quickly came upon two guys that were homeless. We had a chance to share Jesus with them and give them each a Gospel of John. We prayed with them and Todd encouraged them to listen to the Holy Spirit as they read the Word.

> **Your word is a lamp to my feet and a light to my path. -Psalm 119:105**

When reading God's Word, the Holy Spirit begins to shine His light on our path for that day. Let's face it, we live in a dark world and we can all use more light on our paths in order to walk without stumbling. The enemy never stops trying to trip us up. The Apostle Paul reminds us of this in Galatians 5:7, 8…

You ran well. Who hindered you from obeying the truth? This persuasion does not come from Him who calls you.

Satan never relents from trying to get us to fall. We must always be on guard because he is deceptive and very sly, and good at what he does. We must never get to the point that we don't need the Lord's help in our daily living.

The one thing that satan wants all of us to do is stay out of God's Word. He knows the power available to us when we make God's Word the center of our days. We must be careful not to become comfortable and think that *"We've read that Book enough and I already know what it says."* Complacency can cause any of us to fall. In reality, we're all one decision away from heading down a wrong road. That's why the Apostle Paul reminds us in 1 Corinthians 10:12.

Therefore let him who thinks he stands take heed lest he fall.

Just up the road, Todd and I met Javier. He is retired and said that he reads his Bible for about four hours every day. He mentioned the word, *"maranatha"* and expressed how Jesus is coming back again soon. We had a moment to pray with him before we continued riding. It's amazing when you slow down how many people the Lord brings across your path - and each one that comes your way has a unique story.

The riding today was difficult. Hard cross winds and some direct winds in our face smacked us around for most of the day. We also faced some construction sites, so we were forced to ride some miles in the support vehicle rather than on the Interstate. We would find ourselves pedaling through Seligman, Arizona where some say is the birthplace of Route 66.

As we climbed back on the bikes, a husband and wife on the side of the road took time to hand us some apples as we rode by them. Their kind act reminded me of this verse in Proverbs 11:25.

...he who waters will also be watered himself.

When we refresh others, this verse reminds us that the Holy Spirit will then refresh and renew us. Sometimes we can feel so dry and empty because we're storing up everything in us rather than allowing those very blessings to flow through us to "*water*" those around us. If we can learn to slow down and look for ways to hand an apple or glass of water to someone, we may just find ourselves being refreshed as well.

Day 28 - Tuesday, October 3rd

This entire trip has been one where I've been short on sleep and the days have seemed very long. Today, 2:50am seemed way too early to be out of bed. My Fitbit tracks my sleep patterns. Most nights I have a decent percentage of deep, light and REM patterns. I find that most of my days I sleep very sound and feel well rested when I awake. But since the day we landed in Chicago almost a month ago, I don't think my eyes have remained closed past 4:30am. Most days I've been up between 3 and 4am, and I think all the details and logistics of each day are finally catching up to me as my patience is beginning to wear thin. This morning, I'm asking myself, the question,

"Should I ride today or not?"

I chose to ride, even though I really didn't feel like climbing on the bike. It was another frustrating day of riding as the head winds picked up and once again pushed against us. The first twenty-five miles were great as Todd, Joel and I drafted and made great time. But then I found myself falling further and further behind as my energy gave way.

As I pedaled another thirty-seven miles, I found myself alone on a very tight, two-lane road. I kept looking for one of our support vehicles to come by so that I could hop in and head towards the next town. I really needed to get a bite to eat to help regain my strength.

What I also desired was to spend some time biking around Kingman, Arizona and see who I might be able to meet.

Finally, after what seemed a very long time, one of our support vehicles arrived and shuttled me into Kingman. As I made my way around town, a young man came biking towards me and we stopped to talk. He was 32 and I learned that he had spent the last 12 years in prison. He spoke to me about his struggles with drug addiction and how he was raised to follow Christian values but strayed as he became a young adult.

I spoke to him about Christ and he was very willing and eager to pray with me as he re-dedicated his life to the Lord. What a moment as we prayed together! Then the thought hit me! I could've stayed off the bike today or continued biking rather than look for a ride into Kingman. When I ended my day early, I felt discouraged to not push out more miles. But the Lord knew exactly where He wanted me to be. At a convenience store in Kingman, Arizona in the middle of the afternoon to meet a man who needed hope restored in his life! For without hope, life seems meaningless. And there is only one place I know to find such hope.

> ***Now hope does not disappoint, because the love of God has been poured out in our hearts by the Holy Spirit who was given to us. -Romans 5:5***

Maybe you have felt hopeless in the past. Maybe you feel hopeless right now. Take some time and allow God's love to be poured into your heart by the Holy Spirit. May you find hope in Christ when all seems hopeless. He will restore hope if you invite Him into your hopelessness. Just give Him a chance.

This man spent twelve years of his life in what seemed a hopeless situation behind bars. And the only place I had to offer him hope was at the foot of the cross and the empty grave. You see, Christ died for the ungodly, the unrighteous, the forsaken, the hopeless. For you, for me.

> ***For when we were still without strength, in due time Christ died for the ungodly. -Romans 5:6***

Our Only Hope

If you find yourself without strength, you're in a perfect place for God's strength to renew you. I take comfort in these two verses that remind me of where my strength comes from when I am weak.

> ***My grace is sufficient for you, for My strength is made perfect in weakness....For when I am weak, then I am strong. -2 Corinthians 12:9,10***

Don't you love how God is the antithesis of what we are? When we're weak - He is strong. The first part of these verses is an offer from Christ, and the second part a declaration from Paul. It's reassuring to know that Paul found strength in Christ when he was weak, and so can we through the power of Christ and His resurrection.

Don't give up, don't lose hope, don't ever quit. Christ will never give up on you, no matter how hopeless a situation you may find yourself in. He really is only one prayer away.

Arizona...Almost There!

CHAPTER 9
CALIFORNIA, HERE WE COME!

Day 29 - Wednesday, October 4th

"*California here we come!*" He's been saying it for years and we've been hearing it for about a month. Did he ever dream that this would be how it would happen? I don't think so! To his wife, Hilda, or whoever was in earshot, Zjelko would belt it out, *"California here we come!"*

Is it true that the Lord can put dreams or ideas in our hearts a long time before they come to pass? Zjelko and Hilda did not have this trip planned on their calendar. None of us did! But the Lord had it on His calendar and He knew that this team would come together to accomplish His purpose. Was the Lord placing these words on Zjelko's lips for all these years so that when it happened in such an unusual way that the Lord would receive all the glory for it, and not us? I believe so. You see, it would have been easier for Zjelko and Hilda to plan a trip to California by train, plane, or automobile…but not by a bicycle from Chicago! Only the Lord could pull off something like this! I will be forever grateful that He chose this team.

Remember,

> **But God has chosen the foolish things of the world to put to shame the wise, and God has chosen the weak things of the world to put to shame the things which are mighty. -1 Corinthians 1:27**

And because of this,

> **You are worthy, O Lord, to receive glory and honor and power. -Revelation 4:11**

California, the last state on our list. Today we would pedal out of Kingman, Arizona on our way to Needles, California. Temperatures in this part of the country the past several weeks have climbed to 115-120 degrees. Today, we were fortunate as it *"cooled down"* into the 90s.

The ride out of Kingman over Sitgreaves Pass was incredible! We would climb some incredible mountains (3550 ft) which would test our stamina. The climb up the mountain was strenuous, but the ride down the other side was thrilling!

California, Here We Come

On one part of the mountain, I met up with a couple from Germany that we connected with at a previous campground stay. Even though we just met a couple days ago, it felt like I had known Michael and Susanne a lifetime. We chatted a few minutes, took a few pictures and then each went our own separate ways. They mentioned how they would try to be at the Santa Monica Pier on our final day, which would be amazing!

The ride into Oatman, California, has us turn back time to the "*wild, wild west.*" This was a real cowboy town! Hey, the bank even gets "*robbed*" at high noon every day with a "*shootout*" that goes down in the middle of the street. Wild and I'll add - very bold – donkeys that roam the streets greeted us there. One tried to run off with Brian's water bottle while another one tried to chew my handle bar off. It was quite the experience! We took a lunch break in Oatman before continuing our journey down the road.

Zeljko…"*California here we are!!*"

Day 30 - Thursday, October 5th

Today we would leave Needles, California and bike through the desert on our way to a very small town named Ludlow. It was dry and hot with the temperatures reaching (only) into the mid 90's. We were grateful for the "*cooler*" readings on our dashboard compared to a couple weeks ago in this part of the country.

Along the way, Todd and I had a chance to talk with a man from the United Kingdom. He had stopped to help a man who had lost some things off his truck when he decided to go way too fast over some railroad tracks. His name was Steve, and he proclaimed himself an atheist. However, the more we spoke to him and listened to his story, the more I was convinced that the Lord was working in his heart and revealing Himself to Steve.

A few years ago, he found himself going through a very difficult time in his life. He had the painful experience of walking through a divorce, and to try and get away from it all, he flew to Scotland. But how many of you realize, you can't escape your thoughts or problems, no matter how far you try to run away? Remember Jonah?

While in Scotland, this self-proclaimed atheist found his way to a church building where he went inside to just sit and try to find some peace. He shared with us how he sat in silence, admiring the beauty of the building and the stained glass windows. He then turned to us and said, *"I never felt such calm."* It's amazing how *"calm and peaceful"* we feel if we can make room for the Lord in our lives.

I shared this verse with Steve.

Be still and know that I am God. -Psalm 46:10

I then explained to him that what he was experiencing as he sat in this beautiful building was the presence of God. I explained how in the Bible Jesus is called our *"Prince of Peace,"* and how He can calm any storm that we walk through, if we simply place our trust in Him.

As we handed him a Gospel of John, I asked him to let us know if he ever decided to follow Jesus with his life. I was thrilled as he allowed us to pray for him before we pedaled away. What a moment! A self-proclaimed atheist was placed in our direct path and allowed us to pray with him. Once again, the Lord placed someone in our path at just the right time.

Maybe you need peace in your life today. There's only one place that you will find it. The same Jesus who calmed the storm in the Bible wants to calm the storm in you. He may seem like He is far away or sleeping, but one call to Him and He will be there to rescue you before the waters pull you under. You can try other things to try and mask the pain, but they wear off and leave you looking for your next fix. *Jesus is your permanent fix.* There still may be some rough patches and waves to ride out, but He will begin to calm the waves and give you peace beyond your understanding. A big part of finding His peace begins in your mind. Look what the prophet Isaiah reminds us of in his book.

You will keep him in perfect peace, Whose mind is stayed on You, Because He trusts in You. -Isaiah 26:3

You must learn to trust in Him and He will step in and calm the storm around you. You may be feeling overwhelmed and anxious about many things in life. Here is what the Apostle Paul reminds us of in Philippians 4:6, 7.

> ***Be anxious for nothing, but in everything by prayer and supplication, with thanksgiving, let your requests be made known to God; and the peace of God, which surpasses all understanding, will guard your hearts and minds through Christ Jesus.***

Peace is one of the greatest gifts we've been given and I believe it's when we rely on our own understanding that we rob ourselves of experiencing His peace in our lives. Look again at what Paul said above, *"the peace of God, which surpasses all understanding."* When we look at our circumstances, if we dwell on it with our own understanding, it can destroy our peace. But God's peace is meant to transcend or surpass our understanding and replace it with trust in Him and His peace.

We must remember what I read recently that John Ortberg wrote,

> *"Peace does not come by finding a lake with no storms. It comes from having Jesus in the boat."* [1]

So true, we can find peace when all seems unpeaceful. Don't try and figure it out in your own understanding, trust in Him. Get into His Word and He will show you what to do.

> ***Trust in the Lord with all your heart, And lean not on your own understanding; In all your ways acknowledge Him, And He shall direct your paths. -Proverbs 3:5, 6***

There it is again! Don't lean on your own understanding, but rather trust in Him and He will direct your paths. His Word and His Spirit will direct you in all you do, if you just give Him time and get alone with Him.

We ended our day as we rolled into Ludlow, CA. This town, quite literally, has one intersection with a restaurant (that closes around 6pm), a gas station and motel. Thankfully, down the road was a Dairy Queen where we would we would enjoy dinner together. What made the meal even more enjoyable was a conversation I was able to have with two young men. They were very open to discussing the Bible and even prayed with me to re-dedicate their lives to Christ.

California, Here We Come

It was a good way to end the day, and to think - only two more days to go!

Day 31 - Friday, October 6th

We would begin our day on some of the roughest patches of road up to this point. After about 8 -10 miles, the roads would smooth out considerably and we ended the day clocking 87 miles as we enjoyed a gorgeous day on the bikes.

Then another train rolled by and I thought about how I'll miss their sounds, especially when they roll by our team and give a long, loud blow of their whistles. It's like they were encouraging us as we pedaled. Hearing them today reminded me of a time that my wife and I spent the night at a bed and breakfast.

We arrived on a Friday night in Manheim, Pa as we were looking forward to a quiet little getaway. Did I mention *"quiet?"* In our room on our nightstand were a set of ear plugs. Did my wife call ahead and tell them about my snoring? We were really wondering why they were there.

As we went to sleep for the night, we quickly found out the reason for these little sound obstructers. You see, when we first arrived, I noticed that there were train tracks directly across from the B & B. But I asked myself, *"How often (if any) do trains roll down this track?* Answer? About every 45 minutes! This would not have been my first guess. And not only did they go by frequently, it just so happened that there was a crossing directly across the street from where we were staying. And guess what trains are required to do at crossings? Yep, blow their whistle…every hour…all night long! Ah, the reason for the ear plugs! Needless to say, sleep would not come easy that night.

In the morning around the breakfast table, I asked the owner, *"How in the world do you ever get any sleep with the trains running like that all night?"* I'll never forget her answer, as she looked at me and said, "*Oh, we don't even hear them anymore.*" Hmm.

Now the train whistles that we heard while riding our bikes were such an encouragement. Many would blow their horns to kind of say from their engineers seat, *"Keep going!"*

But as I began to reflect back to this night in Manheim, Pennsylvania, I remember thinking to myself that *"If we're not careful, we can become desensitized to sin and the conviction of the Holy Spirit in our lives."* At first, when we're convicted of sin and stop, that's good. But if we don't obey that whistle of conviction to wake up our soul, we can give in to that sin and over time, hardly hear the voice, or whistle of conviction any longer. The more we sin, the more we ignore His voice, the more those whistles will die down and the danger then becomes that we *"Just don't hear them anymore."* We must be careful that we don't become comfortable with our sin and drown out the voice of the Holy Spirit.

James writes about it like this in his book of wisdom.

> **But each one is tempted when he is drawn away by his own desires and enticed. Then, when desire has conceived, it gives birth to sin; and sin, when it is full-grown, brings forth death. -James 1: 14, 15**

Notice the progression: we're tempted *(the whistle sounds)*, then we can either wake up our soul at this point or be drawn away by our own desires and then enticed. Then as that desire is conceived in us, it gives birth, which grows and eventually will bring forth death.

Death? Well, not physical death. Remember when satan told Eve in the garden, *"You won't surely die."* It was a lie! Sure you will. Now we know that it was a spiritual death, not physical. One thing we also must not continue to do is blame everything on the devil. Have you ever heard someone say, *"The devil made me do it."*

No, he didn't, we accomplished it ourselves just fine! I preach a message called, *"The devil didn't make me do it, I did."* The devil doesn't make us do anything. In Christ is found everything we need to overcome the devil's schemes. We have His righteousness, His self-control, His patience. Where we get in trouble is when we try to do everything in our strength, our power, our self-control. My pastor, Paul Grabill, once said, *"It's not in trying harder, but in surrendering more."*

The key to victory is remembering who we are in Christ. James talks about this when he says, *"how can we look in a mirror and forget...."*. Have you ever wondered what James meant by this? I remember hearing Art Thomas teach on this and say that we tend to forget who we are when we stop looking into His mirror, His Word. His Word reminds us who we are and when we forget to take a look in that mirror every day, we can quickly forget what we look like, clothed in His Righteousness.

Don't tune out those whistles in our lives – the ones of encouragement to keep going, but also of conviction to stop the things that could destroy us.

> **Today, if you will hear His voice, do not harden your hearts. -Hebrews 4:7**

> **...exhort one another daily, while it is called "Today," lest any of you be hardened through deceitfulness of sin. -Hebrews 3:13**

While getting our bikes ready for the day, we met Dave, who drove a really nice motorcycle.

Our conversation with Dave was something to behold. He shared with me about when he was a boy he was healed in his feet. He had been rescued out of some very cold waters and the doctors wanted to amputate both feet. But over time, as the doctors began to watch his body heal, they didn't understand just how this was happening. That's when he looked at them and said, *"That's because I have a praying mother."* Oh, the power of a praying mother!

He also began to share with me about a man he saw on the side of the road with a sign that read, *"Jesus abandoned me, anything would help."* Dave said to me that he wanted to stop and tell the man, *"Jesus didn't abandon you, you abandoned Him."* Even as I think about this, my mind goes quickly to the verse in Hebrews 13:5.

> ***For He Himself has said, "I will never leave you nor forsake you."***

This verse is actually a promise from the Old Testament that the Lord God gave to Joshua in Deuteronomy 31:8 and Joshua 1:5. He needed to know that the Lord was going to be with him as he took over leadership from Moses and lead the people into the Promised Land. I'm sure Joshua needed to hear these words, and so do we every day.

Now this quickly turns my heart to the reason of our ride. Yes, this verse says that He will never leave us nor forsake us. That Jesus is always there for us. But throughout the Old Testament, we see God's warning that if we forsake the Lord, that He will forsake us. It's by no means His desire, but a turning away from Him will always bring destruction into our lives…and into our country.

Here is one place that this warning was given.

> ***Now the Spirit of God came upon Azariah the son of Obed. And he went out to meet Asa, and said to him: "Hear me, Asa, and all Judah and Benjamin. The Lord is with you while you are with Him. If you seek Him, He will be found by you; but if you forsake Him, He will forsake you." -2 Chronicles 15:1, 2***

So which is it? Will the Lord *"never leave nor forsake us,"* or will He *"forsake us if we forsake Him?"* Yes!

You see, the Hebrew word for *"forsake"* means to *"release, loosen, allow."* Remember the prodigal son? The father didn't leave his son, he allowed him to go, he loosened and released him, right? The father was waiting for his son to return right where he left him. And so is the Lord with us when we *"come to our senses."* So be careful that you don't walk further away from the Lord and begin to disobey and ignore His promptings. He *will* allow you to leave Him. It's called *"free will."* When people do this, it's very subtle and they barely recognize the distance between them and the Lord at first. But over time, the chasm becomes greater, but always remember, He is waiting for you back home with open arms, even ready to run to you as soon as you turn around and head back.

Let's go back to this verse from Hebrews 13:5 for a moment.

I will never leave you nor forsake you.

Again, this actually was being quoted from the Old Testament. It was spoken by Moses to Israel in Deuteronomy before he died, and then to Joshua by the Lord before he was to enter the Promised land. Yes, if we forsake the Lord, He will forsake (release) us. But if we continue to follow the Lord, we can be guaranteed that He will never leave us nor forsake us.

If you read the entirety of this verse in Hebrews 13:5, the issue being spoken of concerns contentment:

> ***Let your conduct be without covetousness; be content with such things as you have. For He Himself has said, "I will never leave you nor forsake you".***

Here's the bottom line. With Christ in our lives, we should be content and know that He is enough, because He will *"never leave us nor forsake us."*

America has forsaken the Lord, and that is why I believe He has forsaken us. He has allowed us as a nation to walk down our own path and we are reaping some of the consequences of our own actions because of it. And if we do not turn back to the Lord, things will not get any better.

Our Only Hope

Jesus is our only hope. We saw another sign in Oatman, Arizona that once again reminded us of why we were on *"Mission 66."*

This is our only hope, and this is the reason we've been on our bikes for a month now.

> ***...If My people who are called by My name will humble themselves, and pray and seek My face, and turn from their wicked ways, then I will hear from heaven, and will forgive their sin and heal their land. -2 Chronicles 7:14***

It's a great promise, but we must do our part first. He is willing, able and ready to forgive our sin and heal our land, but we must first turn back to Him. I look forward to breaking down this verse in the next several chapters.

Today turned out to be a day where I would spend a majority of the time alone on the bike. For different reasons, the team was spread out in bunches with one, two or three riding together. As I rode past a restaurant, I saw a man sweeping the sidewalks as it looked like they were getting ready to open. As I thought about this man and continued on my ride, the Holy Spirit spoke to my heart, *"Go back and meet him."*

Alvin reminded me of someone who had very little, and in the world's eyes, not much to offer. But in God's eyes we are all so valuable. Alvin was developmentally disabled, but had a heart full of wisdom…and he knew his Bible. He spoke about salvation, trumpets sounding and the skies parting for Christ's return. He even mentioned the places in the Bible that these references were found. And then he said to me, *"Keep pedaling towards your mission…which is eternity!"*

Do you know how glad I was that I obeyed the Holy Spirit and went back to talk with this guy? Alvin truly blessed my day!

So may I say to each of you reading this book in the words of Alvin:

> *"Don't give up, keep going towards your mission…which is eternity."*

California, Here We Come

Or, in the words of the Apostle Paul,

I have fought the good fight. I have finished the race, I have kept the faith. - 2 Timothy 4:7

Someone said this to me the other day, *"It's not in how you start, but rather how you finish."* The Scripture even reminds us of this in Matthew 24:13,

But he who endures to the end shall be saved.

May we determine in our lives not to get sidetracked by the enemy's tricks, but to endure until the very end. One day it will be worth it all when we here these words from our Lord,

Well done, good and faithful servant… -Matthew 25:23

If you live for anything, live for this. Live for the end, not the beginning.

I can't believe it, only one day to go!

Day 32 - Saturday, October 7th

A little over a month ago in Chicago, we pushed away from Lake Michigan and now we are a hundred plus miles from our finish at the Santa Monica Pier! It is only by God's grace that we finished strong. To watch our oldest team member, Zjelko, clock over 100 miles on his bike today was truly remarkable. The Lord has given this man so much strength, truly beyond human comprehension. Like we've been saying for a month now, *"The guy can hardly walk, but he sure can ride a bike."*

Our Only Hope

It has been a challenging journey with a variety of things that would try and stop us from continuing. But I guess any journey of this magnitude is always going to have obstacles to overcome. And with the Lord's help, we overcame!

Over the last thirty-two days, we have seen 15 people make decisions to accept Christ as their Savior and another 12 re-commit their lives to Jesus Christ. We also passed out the message, *"If My People"* to well over a thousand people and placed the Gospel of John into about 70 hands.

My last encounter on the bike almost didn't happen today. I saw a young couple sitting on the sidewalk probably about 20 miles from our finish line. I must admit that I really didn't feel like stopping because the team was ahead of me and we were already past the time that we wanted to arrive at the pier. Daylight hours were fading, but the Lord had to remind me once again, *"This isn't about the bike, it's about the people."*

As I stopped, I learned about a young lady who was 18 and a man, 26. As we sat and talked, they shared with me how they had ran out of gas. I wanted to help them with some cash, but wanted oh so much more for them. The money that they received would help them for a few miles, but the message in the *"Mission 66"* tract and Gospel of John could change their lives forever.

They both said they believed, but I could see and hear the pain on their faces, the hurt in their voices, and especially the scars up and down this young lady's arms. It's hard to cover up your emotions when you're tired and hurting. No matter how much we might say, *"I'm okay,"* deep down we really know if we are, or not. Even when we say we believe, the question then becomes, *"OK, but are we really following Him and His plan with my life?"* We can believe in Jesus and at the same time not be following Him and be very miserable and lost. Remember what James said in his writing?

California, Here We Come

> *You believe that there is one God. You do well. Even the demons believe - and tremble. -James 2:19*

Because demons believe in God, that makes it clear that we must do more than just believe with our head. We must believe in our head, count the cost, accept Christ into our hearts, surrender the entirety of our lives to Him and begin to follow Him. Will we fall short at times, mess up and have to pick ourselves up from time to time? Sure. But I'd rather die trying my best to follow Him than simply say I believe in God in my head and never make it to heaven. Remember this,

> *For by grace you have been saved through faith, and that not of yourselves; it is the gift of God. -Ephesians 2:8*

Don't try to work your way into heaven. Don't try to get into heaven by just believing in your head or going to church on Sunday and think that's your ticket into heaven. Someone once said, *"Many people will miss heaven by 18 inches, the distance between your head and your heart."* [2]

You have been saved by grace through placing your faith, your hope, your life in Jesus Christ. Give your entire life to Christ; let Him take control. You see, we're really not ready to live until we are completely ready to die. And that dying begins by dying to ourselves and giving Him our heart, our lives, well, actually…everything.

As I continued my conversation with this young couple, the young lady took her sunglasses off. As she did, I took mine off as well. She immediately looked at my eyes and said, *"Your eyes remind me of my grandfather's eyes."* I have never had someone compare my eyes to their grandfather's! I'm not really sure what she meant other than the color, but maybe there was something deeper going on there. Maybe her Pap was a believer and encouraged her to really follow the Lord. Maybe I was a reminder of that to her.

With my sunglasses off, I looked in the eyes of this 18-year old girl and felt led to tell her how much Jesus loved her. That she was a princess in God's eyes and that He had great plans for her. As I spoke to her about this unconditional love of Christ, she had tears streaming down her cheeks. I then turned to this young man and

Our Only Hope

spoke to him about the importance of being a godly man and being the spiritual leader in any relationship he may find himself in. I encouraged him to treat this young lady well. I will most likely never see these two here on earth again, but my prayer is that they truly begin to follow Jesus with their lives and they know how deep the Heavenly Father's love is for them.

I trust you know how deep as well.

When we arrived at the Pier, our son, Luke, was there to meet us. He moved to LA about four years ago and it's so rare that we get to be with one another anymore. Just to spend a couple days with he and his new wife Nikki was such a blessing.

The rest of our support team would also be waiting for us as we arrived. We simply could not have done this without such an incredible team of people. *"Thank you"* seems like such a small phrase, but it truly does express how grateful I am for our team!

As we neared the crowds at the Santa Monica Pier, we also noticed our friends from Germany, Michael and Susanne that we met at a campground a few nights back. They were so excited to be there as we ended our journey, and I can't begin to tell you how blessed we were to have them there to greet us as we placed our front tires in the Pacific Ocean. As the waves lapped up against our bikes and shoes, we were elated to be standing at our finish line. This couple may not realize how much it meant to have them there as we concluded our journey. It was hard to say goodbye to them, but we got a few photos, had a prayer, and said our farewells.

California, Here We Come

And so the time has come to say *"farewell"* to you as we near the end of this journey. Before I do, I encourage you to take a moment and reflect on your own journey through life. For some, that may only be a couple decades. For others, it may be several. But no matter how young or old you may be, we must remember that our time on earth is short, and we'll leave this earth before we know it.

I just watched on Facebook Live a pastor friend of mine, Carmen Butler, leading his congregation in the song, *"I'll Fly Away."* One day, if we know the Lord Jesus, guess what? We will fly away! When will that day be? No one knows the day or hour, only our Heavenly Father in heaven. Listen to how the Apostle Paul describes it...

> *For the Lord Himself will descend from heaven with a shout, with the voice of an arch angel, and with the trumpet of God. And the dead in Christ will rise first. Then we who are alive and remain shall be caught up together with them in the clouds to meet the Lord in the air. And thus we shall always be with the Lord. Therefore comfort one another with these words.*
> *-1 Thessalonians 4:16, 17*

Fly away? What a day that will be! Don't miss it. That is our hope. That one-day Jesus Christ will break through the clouds to take us to our eternal home. This life will come to a close.

The chances of you dying are 100%. There will be some when Christ returns that will not die - those will be taken up to meet Him in the sky. Oh, how I hope I'm still alive when He returns! What a day that would be. But if not, one day my time on this earth will have been spent. And the question then becomes, *"How well did I spend it...what did my life really consist of...was it all about me or how I could serve and help others?"*

In my previous book, *"Minutes Matter...Making Every Beat Count,"* I explore some of these questions. Have we all wasted minutes on things that just don't matter? Sure, we all have. But may we strive to live our days with our hope built on Jesus Christ and continue to look for His soon coming return.

You may be thinking, "D*o you really believe this?*" Yes, do you? If not, just ponder this statement I saw on a sign recently.

"ETERNITY IS A LONG TIME TO BE WRONG"

Hey, if I was wrong, I have nothing to lose. But if someone who is an unbeliever was wrong, they have everything to lose. Don't take that chance.

America is in a precarious situation. If we do not turn back to Christ, our nation will continue to unravel and our downfall will be inevitable. Jesus Christ truly is the only hope we have, as individuals and as a nation. When I read through the Old Testament, I see how the people and evil kings *"provoked the Lord to anger."* We must not continue to provoke the Lord to wrath, but rather look to Him and be reminded of the verses that spurred this ride from the very beginning.

> *If My people, who are called by My name, will humble themselves, and pray and seek My face, and turn from their wicked ways, then I will hear from heaven, and will forgive their sin and heal their land. -2 Chronicles 7:14*

Let's do so...before it's too late. Why not take a moment as we end this journey and call upon the Lord God Almighty to forgive our sin and heal our land. It must first begin with His people, humbling ourselves, praying, seeking Him and turning from our wicked ways. Then let's watch how He responds.

CONCLUSION

"You were on a mission, right?"

Sunday mornings in a little town called Centre Hall in the middle of Pennsylvania, I frequently visit a convenience/gas station called "*Sheetz*" for my cup of coffee before I head to the church to get ready for the morning. Over the years, I've gotten to know the people that work there, especially one guy who is there almost every Sunday morning. When we see each other, there are times that we enjoy some good conversation. Following my return to Pennsylvania, I returned to my regular routine of stopping by for my Sunday morning coffee. A bonus is that usually my cup is on the house. I had been gone for five Sundays, and as I walked in and got my coffee, he said to me, *"You were on a mission, right?"*

Then it hit me...aren't we every day? I mean, if we are believers and followers of Christ, our life is a mission trip, right? How many times do we look at a mission trip as going overseas for a week or two, serving in the inner city to the homeless, going to a foreign country, or blocking off some other day on the calendar?

Don't get me wrong, these are all good things to do. But truly, mission trips should begin right where we live. My philosophy on missions is this, if we aren't being a missionary at home, why are we going overseas to be a missionary for just a week or two? Should we be missionaries to other countries? Yes, as the Lord provides opportunity. But it must begin at home.

It's not right to only be a missionary and tell people about the love of Jesus for a week or two out of a year. People are dying all around us every day; right where we live, work and do business. We carry with us the hope and answer that only Jesus Christ can offer them. We must share because really, we are on a mission every day.

Our days fill up so quickly and if not careful, we can miss opportunities the Lord places before us. On the bike trip, we spoke to people on the side of the street, in front yards, in Walmart, McDonalds, in churches, restaurants, campgrounds and a host of other places. So why not look for these opportunities around us every day?

Yes, we were "*on a mission trip.*" But let's make sure we're mindful of the mission trip we are on every day. For Jesus promised He would always be with us when He commissioned His disciples before He returned to His heavenly Father.

> ***Go therefore and make disciples of all the nations, baptizing them in the name of the Father and of the Son and of the Holy Spirit, teaching them to observe all things that I have commanded you; and lo, I am with you always, even to the end of the age. Amen. -Matthew 28:19, 20***

Holy Spirit, fill us, pour out of us and use us to go and be Your witnesses in the world we live in. May we live out our mission trip every day.

And finally, one of the best moments of the trip. I have an amazing wife that loves and supports everything that I do. To be back in her arms is always a highlight of any trip I take, whether it be one night, one week, one month…or even one hour! Baby, you are the best!

Conclusion

Conclusion

BIBLE STUDY

BIBLE STUDY INTRODUCTION

"If My people who are called by My name, will humble themselves, and pray and seek My face, and turn from their wicked ways, then I will hear from heaven, and will forgive their sin and heal their land." 2 Chronicles 7:14

To fully grasp the meaning of a particular verse, a complete reading of the surrounding verses must be read as well. In this very popular verse, some of the questions we must also ask ourselves include:

- What was happening at the time of this writing?
- Who was writing and who are the main characters?
- When was it written and for what reason?

Just what was happening in Israel during this time? Who was the king? Why did God tell His people these things? Well, let's go back and read the entire chapter.

> *When Solomon had finished praying, fire came down from heaven and consumed the burnt offering and the sacrifices; and the glory of the Lord filled the temple.*

And the priests could not enter the house of the Lord, because the glory of the Lord had filled the Lord's house.

When all the children of Israel saw how the fire came down, and the glory of the Lord on the temple, they bowed their faces to the ground on the pavement, and worshiped and praised the Lord, saying: "For He is good, For His mercy endures forever."

Then the king and all the people offered sacrifices before the Lord.

King Solomon offered a sacrifice of twenty-two thousand bulls and one hundred and twenty thousand sheep. So the king and all the people dedicated the house of God.

And the priests attended to their services; the Levites also with instruments of the music of the Lord, which King David had made to praise the Lord, saying, "For His mercy endures forever," whenever David offered praise by their ministry. The priests sounded trumpets opposite them, while all Israel stood.

Furthermore Solomon consecrated the middle of the court that was in front of the house of the Lord; for there he offered burnt offerings and the fat of the peace offerings, because the bronze altar which Solomon had made was not able to receive the burnt offerings, the grain offerings, and the fat.

At that time Solomon kept the feast seven days, and all Israel with him, a very great assembly from the entrance of Hamath to the Brook of Egypt.

And on the eighth day they held a sacred assembly, for they observed the dedication of the altar seven days, and the feast seven days.

On the twenty-third day of the seventh month he sent the people away to their tents, joyful and glad of heart for the good that the Lord had done for David, for Solomon, and for His people Israel.

Thus Solomon finished the house of the Lord and the king's house; and Solomon successfully accomplished all that came into his heart to make in the house of the Lord and in his own house.

Then the Lord appeared to Solomon by night, and said to him: "I have heard your prayer, and have chosen this place for Myself as a house of sacrifice.

When I shut up heaven and there is no rain, or command the locusts to devour the land, or send pestilence among My people,

if My people who are called by My name will humble themselves, and pray and seek My face, and turn from their wicked ways, then I will hear from heaven, and will forgive their sin and heal their land.

Now My eyes will be open and My ears attentive to prayer made in this place.

For now I have chosen and sanctified this house, that My name may be there forever; and My eyes and My heart will be there perpetually.

As for you, if you walk before Me as your father David walked, and do according to all that I have commanded you, and if you keep My statutes and My judgments,

hen I will establish the throne of your kingdom, as I covenanted with David your father, saying, 'You shall not fail to have a man as ruler in Israel.'

"But if you turn away and forsake My statutes and My commandments which I have set before you, and go and serve other gods, and worship them,

then I will uproot them from My land which I have given them; and this house which I have sanctified for My name I will cast out of My sight, and will make it a proverb and a byword among all peoples.

> *And as for this house, which is exalted, everyone who passes by it will be astonished and say, 'Why has the Lord done thus to this land and this house?'*
>
> *Then they will answer, 'Because they forsook the Lord God of their fathers, who brought them out of the land of Egypt, and embraced other gods, and worshiped them and served them; therefore He has brought all this calamity on them.'"*
> *-2 Chronicles 7:1-22*

Forsaking the Lord has grave consequences. We must remember that we cannot forsake the Lord and continue to be blessed by Him. It just doesn't work that way. Solomon became the third king of Israel following his father David. If you remember, David had it in his heart to build the temple, but because he was a man of war, the Lord chose his son, Solomon to do so instead of him.

> *Then King David rose to his feet and said, "Hear me, my brethren and my people: I had it in my heart to build a house of rest for the ark of the covenant of the Lord, and for the footstool of our God, and had made preparations to build it.*
>
> *But God said to me, 'You shall not build a house for My name, because you have been a man of war and have shed blood.'*
>
> *However, the Lord God of Israel chose me above all the house of my father to be king over Israel forever, for He has chosen Judah to be the ruler; and of the house of Judah, the house of my father, and among the sons of my father, He was pleased with me to make me king over all Israel.*
>
> *And of all my sons (for the Lord has given me many sons) He has chosen my son Solomon to sit on the throne of the kingdom of the Lord over Israel.*
>
> *Now He said to me, 'It is your son Solomon who shall build My house and My courts; for I have chosen him to be My son, and I will be his Father.* -1 Chronicles 28:2-6

Chapter 7 of 2 Chronicles contains all that took place in the dedication of the finished temple where God's presence would dwell on earth during that time. The very first verse in this chapter says,

> ***When Solomon had finished praying, fire came down from heaven and consumed the burnt offering and sacrifices and the glory of the Lord filled the temple.***
> ***-2 Chronicles 7:1***

Could you imagine praying and having fire fall from heaven? Pretty powerful prayer! Pretty powerful God! You see, His Presence still wants to fill His temple with His power to equip His people to be His witnesses. When it comes right down to it, that's why we are alive. If you are a believer and follower of Jesus Christ, His Word says we are His temple and the power of the Holy Spirit wants to fill us so that we can be His witnesses. It also says in Acts 1:8 that the Holy Spirit will give us power to be His witnesses. You see, without His power, we are only a "*dim bulb*" rather than a "*bright light.*"

Jesus said,

> ***You are the light of the world...Let your light so shine before men, that they may see your good works and glorify your Father in heaven. -Matthew 5:14, 16***

We are to be His light so that others who are walking in darkness see our good works and come to believe in our Heavenly Father and in His Son, Jesus Christ. We are His temple. Paul reminds us of this when he writes in 1 Corinthians 6:19,

> ***Or do you not know that your body is the temple of the Holy Spirit who is in you, whom you have from God, and you are not your own?***

I find it interesting that Paul asks this question. I wonder if he had to remind them of this because they simply did not know or they forgot and had to be reminded. Maybe this is new to you as well. But when you come to Christ and invite Him into your life, the Holy Spirit comes and takes up residence within you. Now that is amazing!

Our Only Hope

Let's get back to the temple that Solomon built and our study of 2 Chronicles 7:14. The sacrifice that day was great! When the fire descended following Solomon's prayer, it says it *"consumed the burnt offering and the sacrifices."* Could you imagine 22,000 bulls and 120,000 sheep being consumed by fire at one time? That's a big sacrifice! But really, it's nothing compared to the sacrifice that Christ made for us as the Lamb of God.

There was also music at the sacrifice and dedication of the temple. The Levites had instruments and made music to the Lord and the priests sounded the trumpets.

When we come to verse 12 following this sacrifice and dedication, it says...

> ***Then the Lord appeared to Solomon by night, and said to him, "I have heard your prayer, and have chosen this place for Myself as a house of sacrifice."***

Do you know that when we make that decision to follow Christ, He does the same for us today? Notice in that verse you just read, it said that God heard their prayer and chose that place (the temple) for Himself *"as a house of sacrifice."*

We may choose to follow Christ, but in reality, it's Christ who chooses us. Jesus said in John 15:16...

> ***You did not choose Me, but I chose you and appointed you that you should go and bear fruit, and that your fruit should remain, that whatever you ask the Father in My name He may give you.***

And because He chose us and now lives in our body (His temple), our lives then should become a *"house of sacrifice,"* and a consuming fire!

> ***I beseech you therefore, brethren, by the mercies of God, that you present your bodies a living sacrifice, holy, acceptable to God, which is your reasonable service.***
> ***-Romans 12:1***

This is not unreasonable, but rather should be considered normal Christianity. Our *"reasonable service"* to the Lord God Almighty. We are no longer our own. Paul reminds us of this when he continues with these verses from 1 Corinthians 6:20,

> *"or you were bought at a price; therefore glorify God in your body and in your spirit, which are God's.*

To glorify God with our bodies, we must come to grips with the fact that God's Spirit dwells in us and wants to guide and direct all that we say, think and do.

Now when Solomon completed the temple and the Lord God Almighty came to him that night, He said to Solomon,

> *If My people who are called by My name, will humble themselves, and pray and seek My face, and turn from their wicked ways, then I will hear from heaven, and will forgive their sin and heal their land."*
> *-2 Chronicles 7:14*

Just before this, in verse 13, it gives the reason He said this to Solomon.

> *When I shut up heaven and there is no rain, or command the locusts to devour the land, or send pestilence among My people,*

Why would God allow these things to happen to His people? Well, the answer is given towards the end of chapter 7.

> *But if you turn away and forsake My statutes and My commandments which I have set before you, and go and serve other gods, and worship them, then I will uproot them from My land which I have given them; and this house which I have sanctified for My name I will cast out of My sight, and will make it a proverb and a byword among all peoples. -2 Chronicles 7:19, 20*

Notice the *"if"* and *"then,"* the cause and effect. *"If"* His people turned away and served other gods, *"then"* He would uproot them and cast them out of His sight. It was not His will to do this, but rather they choose it and brought it on themselves. One decision always leads to an outcome with the Lord.

But see, there can also be good news when it comes to a cause and effect, *"if and then,"* and this is where we will pick up the study of 2 Chronicles 7:14.

I believe that the United States of America has forsaken the One True God and His statutes and have built other gods in place of Him. Almost a quarter of a millennium since our country was founded, we are at a critical crossroads. Either we turn back to the Lord or we will be cast out of His sight.

You may say, how can you say that? Well, if His people suffered consequences because of their wickedness and idolatry then, may I ask, why wouldn't we now? Does He want to allow that? Of course not. But may we never forget, He is a jealous God. Not in a bad way, but jealous for our affection and first love, because He has our very best interest at heart.

> *For I, the Lord your God, am a jealous God."*
> *-Exodus 20:5(b)*

It's time America takes responsibility of forsaking the Lord and turn back to the only One that can save us from the path of destruction that we've created. Yes, the things He asks of us are not easy, but the benefits are worth every sacrifice. Over the next few chapters we will look closely at the *"ifs"* God asks us to do, and the *"thens"* that He promises to us if we do so.

If My people….

- Will humble themselves
- Pray
- Seek My face
- Turn from the wicked ways

Then…

- I will hear from heaven

- Forgive their sin
- Heal their land

God's Word and promises are true. If we do our part, He will do His. When Jonah proclaimed to Nineveh that they would be destroyed unless they repent and turn from their wickedness, guess what? They repented and one of the greatest revivals of all time broke out in one of the most wicked places of that time.

If it can happen in Nineveh, it can it happen in America! But let's take a close look at each of these points over the next few weeks to see what the Lord desires from His people so that He can then… hear, forgive and heal our land.

LESSON ONE:
IF MY PEOPLE...HUMBLE THEMSELVES

Humility – a modest opinion or estimate of one's own importance.[1]

Let's take a look at some ways God's Word refers to *"humility."*

- *For You will save the humble people, But will bring down haughty looks. -Psalm 18:27*
- *The humble He guides in justice, And the humble He teaches His way. -Psalm 25:9*
- *For the Lord takes pleasure in His people; He will beautify the humble with salvation. -Psalm 149:4*
- *Surely He scorns the scornful, But gives grace to the humble. -Proverbs 3:34*
- *But on this one will I look: On him who is poor and of contrite spirit, And who trembles at My word." -Isaiah 66:2(b)*
- *Jesus said, "...for I am gentle and lowly of heart..." -Matthew 11:29(b)*

Our Only Hope

Now look at what God's Word says about pursuing humility in our lives:

- *...walk worthy of the calling with which you were called, with all lowliness and gentleness..." -Ephesians 4:1(b), 2(a)*

- *Humble yourselves in the sight of the Lord, and He will lift you up. -James 4:10*

- *...be clothed with humility, for God resists the proud, But gives grace to the humble. Therefore humble yourselves under the mighty hand of God, that He may exalt you in due time. -1 Peter 5:5(b,c), 6*

Here is a warning from Christ about exalting oneself, but also a picture of those who choose to humble themselves:

- *And whoever exalts himself will be humbled, and he who humbles himself will be exalted. -Matthew 23:12*

Jesus also had thoughts towards those who are truly humble as he said:

- *Therefore whoever humbles himself as this little child is the greatest in the kingdom of heaven. -Matthew 18:4*

I've heard it said before, *"It's easier to humble yourself than it is to be humbled by someone else...and especially the Lord God Almighty."* I've learned this in my own life the hard way. Pride is the opposite of humility. In Romans 12:3 it reminds us to...

...*not think too highly of ourselves than we ought.*

Pride is something we rarely notice in ourselves but others can see from a mile away. We must be so careful of this making its way into our lives, because *"Pride goes before destruction"* **(Proverbs 16:18).**

The first thing God's people must do according to 2 Chronicles 7:14 to experience healing in our land is to *"humble ourselves."* In America, this does not come easy. We even write songs about how *"proud we are to be an American."* Now don't get me wrong, I'm thankful to live in this land. When traveling to different places around the world, I'm always reminded of how blessed I am to live in America. But in a way, I must ask - have the blessings we've received from the Lord destroyed our humility as a nation? We've forgotten the Lord amidst the abundance of the blessings we possess. Rather than wanting to be great again, we should strive to humble ourselves and be filled with His love.

To be humble begins with confession and a recognition that we are spiritually lost, proud and hopeless without Christ. To have humility realizes the fact that without Christ in our lives we would be a mess and it recognizes that everything we have is from the Lord God Almighty.

The Israelites forgot this, and so has America in many ways. We've drifted from the Biblical truths and have begun to live the way we think is best. Moral truths are disappearing from our society because the Word of God is no longer our moral compass. But I also believe that these moral truths are diminishing in our church culture because of the Word of God being altered or not preached in its entirety. His Word never changes, and neither does its message.

We must remember that what is recorded in 2 Chronicles 7:14 was addressing God's people, *not* those who were His enemies. *We* as God's people must *"humble ourselves"* first and begin to recognize our dependence on Christ, and Christ alone. Not our jobs, our relationships, our IRA's, our bodies, our minds, or our abundance of possessions. No, our dependence must return to Christ. Many gods have taken the place of the One true God in America, just as it happened to those living at the time this verse was written. May this become a prayer of *our* hearts.

> *Humble yourselves in the sight of the Lord, and He will lift you up. - James 4:10*

James, the half-brother of Jesus, had a front row seat at what humility looked like. I think that is why I love his short letter so much. He lived with and watched Jesus grow and model humility. Let us spend time in His Word so that the humility of Christ begins to rub off on us as well.

Small Group Discussion

1) How easy (or how difficult) is it to clothe ourselves with humility in this country that we live in? What gets in the way of this? What must we do to experience true humility?

2) Jesus said that we are to humble ourselves as a "*little child.*" Why do you suppose that He chose a child as an example? Read and discuss **Matthew 18:1-5.**

3) Would you agree that pride is something that is easy to recognize in others, but difficult to see in ourselves? Why or why not? Have you struggled with pride in your own life?

Lesson One

4) James reminds us to "*humble ourselves*" so that He may "*lift us up.*" Read **James 4:7-10**. How can we begin to put this verse into practice?

5) How should God's people respond and how would it look for us to "*humble ourselves?*"

LESSON TWO:
IF MY PEOPLE...PRAY

Prayer is as much about talking with God as it is listening to what He says. Prayer must be two-way communication. Sometimes I can be so focused on what I have to *"say to God,"* when all the while He is trying to say to me, ***"Be still and know that I am God." -Psalm 46:10***

On a recent retreat, I took time to go away by myself and spend time with the Lord. The place I was blessed to be at was called, the *"School House Haven"* in Biglersville, Pa. Once upon a time, back in 1915, this used to be an actual school house. A few years back a wonderful couple purchased it and converted it into a place for those who serve in ministry to come for a time of rest, relaxation and renewal.

I must say, my time there was wonderful as I spent time alone with the Lord. But in reality, I was really never alone because He was right there with me. While at the School House Haven, I found myself saying, *"Speak to me Lord."* And He did - through His Word that was written for me and the Holy Spirit that lives inside of me. You see, I've come to realize that prayer is not only me speaking to Him, but even more so, Him speaking to me.

Our Only Hope

The Lord already knows my deepest needs, my struggles, my fears, my insecurities, my requests. I'm reminded of Psalm 139:16 that says *"There is not a word on my tongue, But behold, O Lord, You know it altogether."* If He already knows the words on my tongue even before I speak them, why is it that I do more speaking than listening when it comes to prayer?

"Speak, Lord, for your servant hears." Remember Samuel? As a child he went to live with Eli, the priest, after his mother, Hannah, promised to give his life back to God.

> *Then the boy Samuel ministered to the Lord before Eli. And the word of the Lord was rare in those days; there was no widespread revelation.*
>
> *And it came to pass at that time, while Eli was lying down in his place, and when his eyes had begun to grow so dim that he could not see,*
>
> *and before the lamp of God went out in the tabernacle of the Lord where the ark of God was, and while Samuel was lying down,*
>
> *that the Lord called Samuel. And he answered, "Here I am!"*
>
> *So he ran to Eli and said, "Here I am, for you called me." And he said, "I did not call; lie down again." And he went and lay down.*
>
> *Then the Lord called yet again, "Samuel!" So Samuel arose and went to Eli, and said, "Here I am, for you called me." He answered, "I did not call, my son; lie down again."*
>
> *(Now Samuel did not yet know the Lord, nor was the word of the Lord yet revealed to him.)*
>
> *And the Lord called Samuel again the third time. Then he arose and went to Eli, and said, "Here I am, for you did call me." Then Eli perceived that the Lord had called the boy.*

> *Therefore Eli said to Samuel, "Go, lie down; and it shall be, if He calls you, that you must say, 'Speak, Lord, for Your servant hears.'" So Samuel went and lay down in his place.*
>
> *Now the Lord came and stood and called as at other times, "Samuel! Samuel!" And Samuel answered, "Speak, for Your servant hears."* -1 Samuel 3:1-10

Did you notice that in the beginning of this chapter it said that *"...the word of the Lord was rare in those days?"* It also stated that *"Samuel did not yet know the Lord, nor was the word of the Lord yet revealed to him."*

Eli, after the third time Samuel came to him, told him to go back and lie down and when this happens again, say, *"Speak, Lord, for your servant hears."* You see, it's not so much our mouths that need to be active in prayer, but rather our ears. We must learn to tune our ears to what the Lord is speaking to us.

As we pray, His Word must become central as we listen to what He says through it and then respond with obedience in our lives. As His Word is revealed to us in prayer, our ears become tuned to the frequency of the Holy Spirit that lives in us and then we begin to walk according to the Lord's will for our lives.

The Bible reminds us to *"Walk in the Spirit, and you shall not fulfill the lust of the flesh."* Galatians 5:16. So we must become more in tune with His Spirit that lives inside of us, and that only happens by spending time in His Word and in His Presence.

Don't get me wrong, there are many facets of prayer including worship, petition, asking for His will to be done, for Christ to meet our needs, seeking forgiveness, forgiving others, to ask Him to deliver us from evil. Jesus taught His disciples how to pray as we see in the Lord's prayer.

> *In this manner, therefore, pray: Our Father in heaven, Hallowed be Your name. Your kingdom come. Your will be done On earth as it is in heaven. Give us this day our daily bread. And forgive us our debts, As we forgive our debtors.*

Our Only Hope

> ***And do not lead us into temptation, But deliver us from the evil one. For Yours is the kingdom and the power and the glory forever. Amen.*** -Matthew 6:9-13

But look what Jesus says right before He teaches and models this prayer for them.

> ***For your Father knows the things you have need of before you ask Him.*** -Matthew 6:8 (b)

When we pray, "***Your Kingdom come, Your will be done On earth as it is in heaven,***" I believe that takes a fine tuning in our hearing to know what the Spirit is saying to us. Take time in prayer and listen for His voice. Allow His Word to guide you into His will to be done on earth, and in and through your life. As we pray, we must learn to listen. Do you hear it? Take time, get into His Word, tune your ear and simply ***"Be still and know that He is God." -Psalm 46:10***

Let us do what Christ reminded the Church in Ephesus in Revelation 2:7,

> ***He who has an ear, let him hear what the Spirit says to the churches.***

If My People…pray! Followers of Jesus: It's time we take time in prayer and hear what the Spirit is saying to us today.

Small Group Discussion

1) **Psalm 46:10** reminds us to *"Be still, and know that I am God."* Why is it so hard to *"be still?"* Can we truly know what God is saying unless we learn to *"be still?"*

2) How did the young boy, Samuel, learn to hear God's voice? What part did Eli play in Samuel knowing, or not knowing, God's voice?

3) **Read Psalm 139 & Matthew 6:7, 8.** In this Psalm, it reminds us that He already knows what we're about to say even before we open our mouths. And Jesus tells us that our Heavenly Father knows all our needs even before we ask Him. So, why do we need to pray?

4) **Read Matthew 6:5-6.** What does Jesus mean when He says that our Heavenly Father will *"reward us openly?"*

5) **Read Matthew 6:25-34.** What are some things that you find in these verses that will help us when we pray?

LESSON THREE:
IF MY PEOPLE...SEEK MY FACE

In this day and age, facial recognition is becoming more popular when it comes to identifying who we are.

The Lord said in 2 Chronicles, **"Seek My face."** What does this look like and how do we do this today? You may have heard it said before, *"We must not only seek His hand, but we must also seek His face."* Seeking His hand is something we do when we have a need. Seeking His face is something we strive after to develop a more intimate and deeper relationship with the Lord.

When the Israelites faced adversity, they sought the Lord's hand and His help. But it seemed to last only a while until they were rescued out of their tough situation and then quickly turned back to their own wicked ways. Seems true even today for many who only *"seek the Lord"* when they find themselves in a difficult situation. And then when things turn around, the Lord is forgotten and all seeking of Him tends to be put aside.

Could it be that God said to *"seek His face"* because in reality He knew that *"to seek His hand"* was a natural thing to do? This can be very true today in the church world as well. When we find ourselves in need of healing or in a tough situation, we can quickly seek His hand. It's not wrong to seek His hand, because He desires for us to come to Him and ask for the needs we have before us. But we must be careful not to quickly forget what He's done. Seeking His face must become a daily pattern so that we remember Him through all the ups and downs of life. When we seek His face, it's long lasting. When we only seek His hand, it's for a quick fix.

To "*seek God's hand*" and to "*seek God's face*" are two very different things. One leaves lasting effects on your life, the other only brings temporary relief. The Lord God Almighty wants to have a very personal relationship with us. Let me explain something from the book of Genesis, the very beginning of time, that should help us grasp how much God wants to be in a close relationship with us.

In the first chapter in Genesis, we see over and over again the name "*God*" used. Here are a few instances:

- ***In the beginning God created... -Genesis 1:1***

- ***And God said, "Let there be light..." -Genesis 1:3***

- ***So God created man in his own image... -Genesis 1:27***

- ***God blessed them... -Genesis 1:28***

But then something is added to His Name in Genesis 2:4 for the very first time. The Bible now refers to God as the "*Lord God.*" Lord "*Yahweh*" in the Hebrew language becomes an additional name for God. Whereas God, "*Elohim*" emphasizes God's greatness and power, now the Name "*Yahweh*" is added to God's Name to emphasize the more personal Name He desires for us to know Him by. You see, God is not only the One who created the heavens and the earth, but He is also the Lord God who desires to have a real, personal relationship with us through His Son, Jesus Christ.

I like how my "*Full Life Study Bible*" describes this fact. And I really like how they describe what it means when you see the words "*Lord God*" used together.

"Where the words 'Lord God' are coupled together, they point to God as the all-powerful Creator who has entered into a caring covenant relationship with humankind."[1]

Lesson Three

Yes, when 2 Chronicles 7:14 reminds us to *"seek His face,"* the Lord God is reminding us that He desires us to know Him personally and intimately. Not only as God who created the universe and everything we see, but it's so humbling to think that He also desires us to know Him as we seek Him.

Here are some other places throughout the Bible that mentions seeking the Lord.

- *But from there you will seek the Lord your God, and you will find Him if you seek Him with all your heart and with all your soul. -Deuteronomy 4:29*

- *If you seek Him, He will be found by you; but if you forsake Him, He will forsake you. -2 Chronicles 15:2*

- *But those who seek the Lord shall not lack any good thing. -Psalm 34:10*

- *Seek the Lord and His strength; Seek His face evermore! -Psalm 105:4*

- *Blessed are those who keep His testimonies, Who seek Him with the whole heart. -Psalm 119:2*

- *I love those who love me, and those who seek me diligently will find me. -Proverbs 8:17*

- *Seek the Lord while He may be found, Call upon Him while He is near. -Isaiah 55:6*

- *And you will seek Me and find Me, when you search for Me with all your heart. -Jeremiah 29:13*

- *For it is time to seek the Lord, Till He comes and rains righteousness on you. -Hosea 10:12(b)*

- *Seek the Lord, all you meek of the earth, Who have upheld His justice. Seek righteousness, seek humility. -Zephaniah 2:3(a)*

- *But seek first the kingdom of God and His righteousness, and all these things shall be added to you. -Matthew 6:33*

- *But without faith it is impossible to please Him, for he who comes to God must believe that He is, and that He is a rewarder of those who diligently seek Him. -Hebrews 11:6*

These verses speak of the importance of seeking a personal relationship with the Lord God Almighty. We can only have that once we commit our lives to Jesus Christ and make Him Lord of our lives. Here is where it begins.

...that if you confess with your mouth the Lord Jesus and believe in your heart that God raised Him from the dead, you will be saved. -Romans 10:9, 10

Have you believed? Have you made Him the Lord of your life? Have you confessed Him with your mouth? Not just in an initial prayer to receive Him into your heart, but confessed Him and shared with others that Jesus is now Lord of your life?

You see, God wants us to have a relationship with Him. Saying you *"go to church"* is one thing. Don't get me wrong, we should worship together on Sundays with the Body of Christ. But too many think that walking through church doors will also gain them entrance through heavens doors. No, it's only through Jesus that we are saved and have access to heaven one day. You see, Jesus is the door.

I am the door. If anyone enters by Me, he will be saved, and will go in and out and find pasture. -John 10:9

Let's make sure we're seeking His face and not simply His hand.

Lesson Three

Small Group Discussion

1) The Israelites were told to "seek His face." Do you believe that they sought His hand more than they did His face? Is so, could this be the reason they always fell in and out of a relationship with the Lord God Almighty?

2) What do you see as the difference between seeking the Lord's hand as compared to seeking His face? Which is easier or comes more natural? Why is that?

3) **Hebrews 11:6** says that *"He is a rewarder of those who diligently seek Him."* What do you think it means to *"diligently"* seek the Lord and in what ways do you think He rewards those who do so?

4) How and when did you make Jesus the Lord of your life? Take time and share your testimony with one another.

LESSON FOUR:
IF MY PEOPLE...TURN FROM THEIR WICKED WAYS

Here are some definitions of Repentance:

- Goes beyond feeling to express distinct purposes of turning from sin to righteousness; the Bible word used most often translated *"repentance"* means a change of mental and spiritual attitude toward sin.[1]

- To turn from sin and dedicate oneself to the amendment of one's life. Sincere regret or remission.[2]

The Israelites had trusted in other gods and forsaken the One True God. At the end of 2 Chronicles 7 it says,

> ***And as for this house, which is exalted, everyone who passes by it will be astonished and say, 'Why has the Lord done thus to this land and this house?' Then they will answer, 'Because they forsook the Lord God of their fathers, who brought them out of the land of Egypt, and embraced other gods, and worshipped them and served them; therefore He has brought all this calamity upon them. -2 Chronicles 7:21, 22***

Our Only Hope

You see, the Israelites brought all this upon themselves because they stopped seeking the Lord and began to chase after all types of other gods. We must remember that we will become by-products of the things we chase after. Whatever we seek and pursue more than Jesus Christ can quickly will become our idol and god over time. As God's people, we must begin to ask the very hard question, *"Do I really love the Lord God with all my heart, soul, mind and strength?"*

At first thought, we may quickly say "Y*es, of course.*" But we must look deep inside ourselves and ask, *"Do I really? Is there anything that I love more than You? Anything?"*

And we must remember that your *"anything"* may look totally different than someone else's *"anything."* We must be careful not to force our convictions upon others because they may not struggle in the same ways we do. A relationship, a job, a habit or addiction, money, comfort, pleasure in sin, hobbies…the list goes on and on. Note, not all other *"gods"* are bad in and of themselves. We know addictions are bad and can become *"gods"* in our lives. But so can relationships, when we place people above the Lord God and make that person a *"god"* to us. May we never make a human being an idol or a god. Why? Well, simply put, they're human. We all, as you know, have *"feet of clay."*

Feet of clay – a weakness or hidden flaw in the character of a greatly admired or respected person.[3]

The last thing 2 Chronicles 7:14 tells us we must do to see revival happen is repentance. We must turn away from the things that have taken the place of God in our lives. If it is blatant sin (addictions, habits, sexual sin, etc.), we must confess it, repent of it and get it out of our lives.

If it is something that is not blatant sin, but out of balance in our lives (relationship, a job, money, etc), we must confess to it being out of balance and it being a *"god"* and seek His forgiveness. Don't immediately quit the job, end the relationship or burn all your money. No, simply ask the Lord to help you bring them into the right balance under the Lordship of Jesus Christ.

Repentance, turning from our wicked ways, is a difficult thing because of our sinful nature that always wants to try and come alive again and pull us down. We must always be on guard against the enemies attempts to lure us back down this path. Don't ever get too comfortable as you walk with the Lord. Remember what Paul wrote to the Corinthian church,

> *Therefore let him who thinks he stands take heed lest he fall. No temptation has overtaken you except such as is common to man... -1 Corinthians 10:12, 13*

But I love the next part of verse 13…

> *…but God is faithful, who will not allow you to be tempted beyond what you are able, but with the temptation will also make the way of escape, that you may be able to bear it.*

Now let's take a look at the amazing benefit that comes with true repentance.

> *Repent therefore and be converted, that your sins may be blotted out, so that times of refreshing may come from the presence of the Lord. -Acts 3:19*

Want to be refreshed, renewed by the Lord Jesus Christ? Today's your day!

Small Group Discussion

1) What prevents us from truly repenting? What gets in our way?

2) Is it true that we become by-products of the things we chase after? Is this hard to see in ourselves? How can having an accountability partner help us in this way?

3) Take a hard look inside, is there anything you love more than Jesus? If so, take time, pray and repent.

4) Read these verses from **Acts 3:19** again and discuss how these verses can change your life.

LESSON FIVE:
THEN...I WILL HEAR FROM HEAVEN

I would assume that most everyone reading this realizes that our sin separates us from God. That is why Christ had to come and die for our sin, so that we could be reconciled to God.

But our sin also causes God to not be able to hear us when we pray. Sin puts a barrier between us and God. Look what the prophet Isaiah writes in chapter 59, verse 2.

> *But your iniquities have separated you from your God; And your sins have hidden His face from you, So that He will not hear.*

Now, first of all, I realize that none of us are perfect. Our flesh will continue to struggle with temptation and sin after we are saved. I don't believe that every time we sin, that God's ears get plugged up and He doesn't hear. What I do believe is that when we willfully and with full knowledge live in habitual sin, it causes our prayers to be hindered. The writer of Hebrews puts it like this.

> *For if we sin willfully after we have received knowledge of the truth, there no longer remains a sacrifice for sins.*
> *-Hebrews 10:26*

Even Peter talked about how husbands can cause their prayers to be hindered when we don't live in an understanding way with our wives.

> *Husbands, likewise, dwell with them with understanding, giving honor to the wife, as to the weaker vessel, and as being heirs together of the grace of life, that your prayers may not be hindered. -1 Peter 3:7*

We must be careful because there are things that can hinder our prayers, or even cause them to be not heard at all. But when we do the previous things we studied in the past few lessons, it's like the heavens are opened and God bends His ear towards us once again.

Want to always have your prayers heard? Live in a right relationship with the Lord God and be sensitive to the Holy Spirit when He convicts you of sin. And when He does, take a moment, confess, repent, receive His forgiveness, don't live under condemnation, and move forward. That is the whole premise of Romans 8:1 which says,

> *There is therefore now no condemnation to those who are in Christ Jesus, who do not walk according to the flesh, but according to the Spirit.*

Most people know the first part of this verse, but the second part is vitally important. We must walk according to the Spirit, not the flesh, so the condemnation that the devil wants to put on us when we "mess up" does not stick to us.

There is nothing more satisfying to know that when we pray, God hears our prayers. When we humble ourselves, pray, seek His face and turn from our wickedness, we are guaranteed from God's Word that He will hear our prayers from heaven.

Here are a few things that the Psalmist reminds us of concerning prayer:

- *Hear me when I call, O God of my righteousness! You have relieved me in my distress; Have mercy on me, and hear my prayer. -Psalm 4:1*

- *The Lord has heard my supplication; The Lord will receive my prayer. -Psalm 6:9*

- *Hear a just cause, O Lord, Attend to my cry; Give ear to my prayer which is not from deceitful lips. -Psalm 17:1*

- *I have called upon You, for You will hear me, O God; Incline Your ear to me, and hear my speech." -Psalm 17:6*

- *Give ear, O Lord, to my prayer; And attend to the voice of my supplications. In the day of trouble I will call upon You, For You will answer me. -Psalm 86:6, 7*

All these prayers came from the heart and mouth of David. He cried out to God and was confident that He was there to hear and answer his prayers. And so can we. David, a man after God's own heart, had many things he needed to clear up and repent of. And when he did, God certainly heard his prayers.

I'm reminded of the verse in Hebrews that tells us to come boldly to the throne of grace.

> **Let us therefore come boldly to the throne of grace, that we may obtain mercy and find grace to help in time of need. -Hebrews 4:16**

How can we come boldly before the throne of grace? Only because of what Jesus did for us. The writer of Hebrews reminds us of this right before the verse you just read.

> **Seeing then that we have a great High Priest who has passed through the heavens, Jesus the Son of God, let us**

> *hold fast our confession. For we do not have a High Priest who cannot sympathize with our weaknesses, but was in all points tempted as we are, yet without sin.*
> *-Hebrews 4:14, 15*

We can come boldly because Jesus overcame every temptation we will ever face. When we fail, He is there to sympathize with our weaknesses, but then remind us to come boldly back to His throne to receive His grace.

Small Group Discussion

1) What are some things that may be hindering your prayers right now? The hard part is admitting them. The enemy wants us to be quiet about them and to keep them a secret. But when we open our mouths and confess, then comes freedom!

2) **Isaiah 59:2** says that our sins cause the Lord to hide His face from us. What do you think it means that *"He will not hear?"* How does this reconcile with the fact that God is Omniscient, *"all knowing"*?

3) The Psalmist, David, cried out to God and knew his prayers were heard. However, there were consequences that David lived with the rest of his life. With this in mind, how do we *"no longer live under condemnation"* and be confident as we go boldly to the throne of grace? Read **Romans 8:1** and **Hebrews 4:16.**

4) Take a look at some of David's prayers. Which ones can you relate to the most in your life? Why?

LESSON SIX:
THEN...I WILL FORGIVE THEIR SINS

Once the air is cleared, forgiveness is found. To be forgiven of sin is the greatest gift we can ever receive. This benefit will come to God's people as we humbly come before Him. It's not like God only chooses to forgive some of our sins, He freely forgives all our sins. And not only does He forgive them, He forgets them.

> *As far as the east is from the west, So far has He removed our transgressions from us. -Psalm 103:12*
>
> *You will cast all our sins into the depths of the sea. -Micah 7:19*

But the key is we must admit that we have sinned.

> *If we say that we have no sin, we deceive ourselves, and the truth is not in us. If we confess our sins, He is faithful and just to forgive us our sins and to cleanse us from all unrighteousness. If we say that we have not sinned, we make Him a liar, and His Word is not in us."*
> *-1 John 1:8-10*

Our Only Hope

Sin is what will keep us out of heaven. That's why the blood of Jesus was shed at the cross - for our sins - to cleanse us from all our unrighteousness. We become *"righteous,"* in right standing before God when we are forgiven.

Notice the Lord says in 2 Chronicles 7:14, ***"I will forgive their sin."*** Period! Not certain sins, not just the ones that are really bad, or even not so bad. Not just the good things we're supposed to be doing but choose not to. Remember what James reminds us of:

> ***...to him who knows to do good and does not do it, to him it is sin. -James 4:17***

The great news is that Jesus Christ forgives all our sin. Only sin can separate us from God. Someone who has not accepted Christ and has never asked to be forgiven is still living in sin and should they die in this state will be eternally separated from the Lord God Almighty. Again, only sin will separate us from eternity in heaven.

But once you ask Him to forgive you and you've accepted His death on the cross as payment for your sins, you're forgiven! At this point, nothing can separate us from His love. Paul reminds us of this when he writes,

> ***For I am persuaded that neither death nor life, nor angels nor principalities nor powers, nor things present nor things to come, nor height nor depth, nor any other created thing, shall be able to separate us from the love of God which is in Christ Jesus our Lord. -Romans 8:38, 39***

His death was the final payment for your sins. One of the statements Jesus cried out while on the cross was, ***"It is finished."*** He didn't mean His life. What He meant was payment for our sins was completely paid in full, finished.

The Greek word that Jesus cried out was *"tetelestai."* It means, *"It is finished,"* or *"paid in full."* This word back in Jesus' day was stamped upon a receipt when someone would pay off a debt in full. It was a word that those standing by the cross recognized when they heard it. *"Paid in full!"* The sin of the world was *"paid in full."* We owed a debt we could not pay, He paid a debt He did not owe. That's the reason the Roman soldier cried out at the cross, **"Truly this was the Son of God."** (Matthew 27:54)

To be debt free is a blessing. If you have ever paid off a car or a mortgage you know the feeling of being free of that debt!!

But imagine that you owed $100,000 on your mortgage and someone came to your home, knocked on your door and said, *"Here is $100,000 cash, I would like to pay off your mortgage."* Would you would close the door and say, *"No thank you?"*, or swing it wide open, jump for joy and shout "H*allelujah!"* Yes, we may not feel worthy to receive such a gift, but that's why it's called amazing grace.

When I shared this illustration one Sunday in a sermon, one man who I had come up front to play the part of the home owner said he would feel *"Like he was not worthy to receive such a gift and maybe give it to someone else who has a greater need."* That made me stop and think. Then I said, "O*k, imagine this person had a $100,000 check for every person in the world, would you receive it then?"* He smiled and said, *"Yes."*

> **Behold, I stand at the door and knock. If anyone hears My voice and opens the door, I will come in to him and dine with him, and he with Me. -Revelation 3:20**

Jesus spoke these words to the church in Laodicea in one of his seven letters to the churches. This was the church that was neither *"hot nor cold,"* but rather *"lukewarm."* And because of this the Bible states that Jesus said he would *"vomit"* them out of His mouth. Yes, vomit! Pretty strong words. That is why He said to them just before this verse above,

> **Therefore be zealous and repent. -Revelation 3:19**

Most of the times we think of zealous in other ways, like being zealous with our faith. But this church was told to be zealous in their repentance. Because they had lukewarm faith, they were told to be

Our Only Hope

zealous and repent. We must do the same if this is true in our personal lives and within our churches as well.

Jesus died to pay off our debt in full. And not only for you, but for everyone in the world. I met a guy on this bike trip who said, *"I've done so much wrong, He could never forgive me and I could never ask Him to."* It was a sad moment. He could not come to grips with the fact that Jesus wanted to forgive even the most sinful things that he had ever done. Jesus died for this man and for every person that ever lived. Will He forgive our sin when we cry out to Him? You better believe it!

Lesson Six

Small Group Discussion

1) Do you ever struggle with knowing that Christ has forgiven all your sin? Is it hard for you to receive such amazing grace with all you've done in your past?

2) Does condemnation ever hold you back or weigh you down? Read **Romans 8:1** in its entirety and discuss what this actually means. How can we be set free from condemnation? How can we walk according to the Spirit and not according to the flesh?

Our Only Hope

3) Read **Romans 8:38, 39**. What does Paul mean that nothing *"shall be able to separate us from the love of God which is in Christ Jesus our Lord?"*

4) Have you been forgiven? Have you asked Christ to forgive you of all your sin? If so, be confident and walk according to His Spirit that now lives in you. If you haven't, there is no better time than right now.

LESSON SEVEN:
THEN...I WILL HEAL THEIR LAND

Heal our land...more than ever do we need this. So many people view the health of our land by what the stock market is doing and how our economy is performing. If the unemployment rate is low and stock market is high, well - we must be doing ok, right? Or could it mean that we have a *"love and obsession"* for money in this country?

Timothy reminds us about the love of money.

> *...the love of money is a root of all kinds of evil.*
> *-1 Timothy 6:10*

But that is our country. What about in the church, amongst God's people? Remember, this text from 2 Chronicles 7:14 begins with God saying, *"If My people."* Not the world, not those that aren't believers, not the government, not the country. No, it begins with *His people*, it begins with *us*.

Our land is in desperate need of spiritual healing. We have killed millions of babies and passed laws to support it. We've taken prayer and Bible reading out of our schools and wonder why our schools are falling apart. We are trying to re-define the marriage covenant that God established from the beginning of time between one man and one woman. This is just scratching the surface of what our country has done by turning their backs on God, but it's a pretty deep scratch.

"I will heal their land." I must admit to sometimes thinking, *"Have we fallen too far? Have we forsaken the Lord so much and is there still hope?"* This I do know, Jesus is our only hope. It's why I entitled this book, *"Our Only Hope."* Unless America turns back to the Lord, there is no hope.

And it begins with God's people. We must begin to cry out and seek Him like never before. Revival, a return to Biblical values, is God's desire. For we know that in 2 Peter 3:9 it says that He is **"Not willing that any should perish but that all should come to repentance."** Sometimes I wonder how many churches are even preaching this message today?

May we repent for our sins, and also for the sins of our country. I'm reminded of how Moses cried out for the sins of the people when God wanted to destroy them because of their sin and rebellion against Him. Take a look at this scene from the book of Exodus. It is right after the Israelites gave Aaron, Moses brother, their gold and *"out popped"* a golden calf for them to worship. Moses was taking a long time up on the mountain as he was meeting with the Lord. Then the Lord spoke to him.

> *Go, get down! For your people whom you brought out of the land of Egypt have corrupted themselves. They have turned aside quickly out of the way which I commanded them. They have made themselves a molded calf, and worshipped it and sacrificed to it, and said, "This is your god, O Israel, that brought you out of the land of Egypt." And the Lord said to Moses, "I have seen this people, and indeed it is a stiff-necked people! Now therefore, let Me alone, that My wrath may burn hot against them and I*

> *may consume them. And I will make of you a great nation." -Exodus 32:7(b)-10*

What an offer Moses had on the table! The Lord would get rid of these people and start a new nation with him. Hmm...pretty tempting, I'd say. But look what Moses does next:

> ***Then Moses pleaded with the Lord his God, and said: "Lord, why does Your wrath burn hot against Your people whom You have brought out of the land of Egypt with great power and with a mighty hand? Why should the Egyptians speak, and say, 'He brought them out to harm them, to kill them in the mountains, and to consume them from the face of the earth.'? Turn from Your fierce wrath, and relent from this harm to Your people." -Exodus 32:11, 12***

And then look what it says a little further down.

> ***So the Lord relented from the harm which He said He would do to His people. -Exodus 32:14***

The Lord relented as Moses cried out to Him for His people. Mercy, grace...what gifts from the Lord.

Believers and followers of Jesus Christ, may we begin to cry out for our country. But may we first cry out for repentance in our own lives as well. Our only hope for our land to be healed is Jesus and a return to the Word of God. When Josiah, the youngest king ever, found the Book of the Law, he began to clean house. Here are a few verses concerning what God's people did when God's Word was discovered.

> ***And he read in their hearing all the words of the Book of the Covenant which had been found in the house of the Lord. Then the king stood by a pillar and made a covenant before the Lord, to follow the Lord and to keep His commandments and His testimonies and His statutes, with all his heart and all his soul, to perform the words of***

> *this covenant that were written in this book. And all the people took a stand for the covenant.* -2 Kings 23:2,3

Church, it's time we also take a stand. As they found the Word of God, they made it a priority and asked for God's forgiveness. The king made a covenant to follow the Lord and His ways with all his heart and soul, and the people followed suit. We must also do the same. For Jesus Christ and a return to His Word is truly *our only hope*!

> *If My people who are called by My name, will humble themselves, and pray and seek My face, and turn from their wicked ways, then I will hear from heaven, and will forgive their sin and heal their land.* -2 Chronicles 7:14

Lesson Seven

Small Group Discussion

1) Our land needs healing. What are your thoughts on the condition of the church, not our country? Remember, revival happens with God's people.

2) Has the church gotten away from God's Word? Is the Bible still taught and preached like it once was in our churches?

3) Read **2 Kings 23:2,3** and describe how the king and the people both made a covenant and what they desired to do to come back to the Lord with all their heart and soul.

   a. Read and discuss what Jesus said was the greatest commandment in **Mark 12:28-34.**

4) Moses cried out to God and interceded for His people. We must ask ourselves how much time do we pray and intercede for His people to come back into a right relationship with Him. How hard is this to do and how should this look in our life?

5) Read **2 Chronicles 7:14.** After studying this verse over the past several weeks, how has your view of this verse changed you?

Bibliography

Chapter 2:

1. George Wood. General Council of the Assemblies of God. Article: *"Called to Serve."*

Chapter 7:

1. *The Princess Bride* (1987) Film. Produced by: Andrew Scheinman; Rob Reiner. Production Company: Act III Communications.

Chapter 9:

1. John Ortberg (2009). *"The Me I Want To Be"*, p.116, Harper Collins. "Peace does not come by finding a lake with no storms. It comes from having Jesus in the boat."

2. Paul W. Empet (September 2012). Publisher: Crossway. Tract: Missing Heaven By 18 Inches. "Many people will miss Heaven by 18 inches."

Lesson #1:

1. 2019 Dictionary.com. Definition: Humility – modest opinion or estimate of one's own importance.

Lesson #3:

1. Donald C. Stamps, General Editor. Life Publishers International; 1992. The Full Life Study Bible.

Lesson #4:

1. 2019 Dictionary.com. (Century Dictionary). Repentance goes beyond feeling to express distinct purposes of turning from sin to righteousness; the Bible word used most often translated "repentance" means a change of mental and spiritual attitude toward sin.

2. 2019 Merriam-Webster Dictionary. Definition, Repent: To turn from sin and dedicate oneself to the amendment of one's life. Sincere regret or remission.

3. 2019 Dictionary.com. Definition, Feet of Clay: a weakness or hidden flaw in the character of a greatly admired or respected person.

ABOUT THE AUTHOR

K.R. Mele's greatest calling and joy since he gave his life to Christ has been as a husband and father. Married for thirty one years, he and his wife, Gina, reside in Centre Hall, Pennsylvania and have two children. Their son, Luke and his wife Nikki reside in California. Their daughter, Olivia and her husband TJ live in Florida.

K.R. served as Children's Pastor in two churches before his family planted *Family Life of Penns Valley* in Central Pennsylvania. Both he and Gina are involved in overseas work with *Haven of Hope Global Ministries*.

K.R. published his first book **Don't Quit** in 2015 and a second book in 2018 entitled **Minutes Matter...Making Every Beat Count.** He also began an evangelistic biking ministry, **Rock-n-Roll Ministries,** and has twice led cross-country bicycle missions trips.

Learn more about Rock-n-Roll Ministries and K.R.'s two previous books at www.rocknrollministries.com.

www.ingramcontent.com/pod-product-compliance
Lightning Source LLC
LaVergne TN
LVHW051519070426
835507LV00023B/3189